Abstract Realism

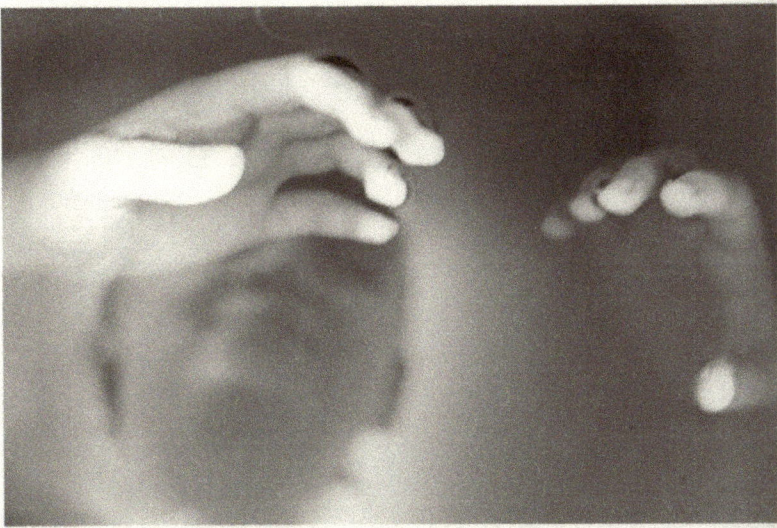

~ true stories ~

By

Alexis Nichele

1

ISBN# 978-0-6151-6820-3

Table of Contents

Abstract Realism ˜ The Movie script excerpts

Forward

Abstract Realism is a book of true paranormal, telepathic, telekinetic, psychic and other-worldly experiences. The experiences are all mine and all true. I have compiled many strange and sometimes frightening experiences into this book as well as some of my art, photographs, poetry, and social ideologies. I've titled this book Abstract Realism because the truth is stranger than fiction and although true, these experiences are so incredible they seem as if they are fiction. I have dated many of the experiences though they are not all in sequential order. I have also written some of the experiences in a script format because it is sometimes easier and more fun to read, understand and follow. I have placed most of the movie script at the end of the book however these are just excerpts of the script and not the entire script. I want this book to be fun, enlightening and as unique as its contents and writer.

So often in life we become distracted from truth and magic. I am writing this book because I am tired of telling these same experiences (which I call stories) over and over again yet feel that they are very amazing and important. I want to share them. I must share them! I also must warn you that these stories are out of the ordinary and to the unaware possibly frightening. I guarantee that it is not my intention to give you nightmares. However, if you have a narrow perception of reality this book could be very disturbing to you. Otherwise you will more than likely truly enjoy this wildly strange book about my life as Alexis.

Aside from the many incredible experiences which I have written about in this book, there is much I have left out. Not only am I a great story-teller but I am also often very psychic and have predicted many things. I had a premonition about 9/11 the night before it happened. I predicted the war in Iraq years before it actually occurred. A friend of mine had went to prison nine months before September 11th and I remember telling him that he would be safer in prison because we would be going to war soon. Of course he had no idea as to what I was saying but neither did most people at that time. Everyone would just brush me off as usual. I also remember having a conversation with two young men while working on the T.V. show Dharma and Greg. I was telling the two young men that we would be going to war soon. The two young men were 19 year old cousins. One of the guys proceeded to argue with me and tell me that I was wrong. I told him that I was not wrong, he was just not paying attention. The conversation had gotten somewhat heated and eventually the prop guy came over and said, "come on you two we are all happy people here." my response of course was, "no, we are not". They all pretty much just thought I was just some crazy black girl with the exception of the young man's cousin, who listened and agreed with my opinion. I would like to thank him. Well, three weeks later George W. got on television and told us that we were at war. I often wonder what they all think of this crazy black girl now. ☺

I am also a healer and although I have never practiced ReiKi, I have naturally healed two different people on separate occasions of their migraine headaches without touching them. I have only attempted this kind of thing on rare occasions when I know that there is no doubt in my mind of my abilities and still I am always truly surprised when it works.

So you see, although I am just as human and imperfect as everyone else, I am an extraordinary being with many different talents and abilities. I hope that you find this book exciting and inspiring. May the truth set us free and may The Creator bless us all.

Introduction

I was born in Santa Monica California and raised in Hollywood. I am a true Hollywood native. My mother named me Alexis after Alexis Smith, an actress and Nichele Nichols of Star Trek fame. I began freaking people out at three months of age. My mother told my grandmother that I was saying Hi to people. Of course grandma didn't believe her until one month later when we went to visit her in Chicago for my 1st Christmas. Grandma was holding me, she looked at me and said, "hi Alexis". I looked at her and responded with a long "hiiiiii" and a smile. Grandma yelled, "oh my God this girl does say hi!"

When I was 18 months I almost died of viral meningitis and had to have a spinal tap. I spent two weeks in the hospital. As a side effect of the meningitis I had migraine headaches from the age of two to twelve. In the summers I would get them every other day. There was no medication for migraines back then so I would just scream and cry for hours with a wet towel on my head. When I was twelve I woke up one day and knew that the migraines were gone and would never return. That was the same year I met Arnold. I have not had one migraine since. I am currently 30.

Clarence Paul and Stevie Wonder

My Dad, Clarence Paul was Motown A&R, he produced and wrote many of Stevie Wonder's first albums. Dad's brother Lowman Pauling started the first ever soul group. He has also been credited with inventing distortion and feedback for electric guitars and fuzz bass. I act a little and I also sing Rock. I am a girl and have dredlocks so its quite a sight and sound my voice is deep like my dad's and uncle's voices. My Godfather was Marvin Gaye although he died when I was seven.

I grew up on film and T.V. sets because my mom worked in film and television in the 80's and 90's. She worked for Dinah Shore in the early 80's and would often take me to the set with her. I remember meeting the chimp from the T.V. show BJ and the Bear. We were the same height and color and I think he decided I was his girlfriend because he grabbed my hand and walked around the set with me for a long time. I'll never forget that. Mom also worked for Ivan Reitman for many years. Ivan actually introduced me to Arnold Schwarzenegger just before shooting began on the movie Twins.

Growing up in Hollywood was cool until 1984. Before then we were able to walk around freely and no one would harass us kids. My good friend Josh and I would ride our bikes to Griffith Park and Hollywood

Blvd. Once we found a woman's body in the bat cave but the boys wouldn't let me look so I'll never know if it was true. Josh and I are like brother and sister. We walked to the school bus together everyday. Until I was 16 I had to be up before the sun to get to the bus. In high school I had a stalker. Anyway, by the time I was ten or eleven all of the kids we had grown up with got into gangs and began to terrorize us. At the same time our apartments were being taken over by roaches. I would try to sleep standing up because the bugs would crawl on me while I slept. I was a nervous wreck. I didn't want to be inside because of the bugs and I didn't want to go outside because of the gangs. My mom decided it was time to move. My mom asked her boss Ivan to help and we moved to North Hollywood. That's were I met my stalker and the first of the bullies I'd have to deal with. Ironically the stalker and the girls' who consistently threatened me, lived in the same building right next door to our building. Not fun but easier to deal with than the gangs and shootings. All throughout my education girls were after me for this reason or that. One of the reasons I left Clark University was because of harassment. One month before leaving Clark U, I began having dreams where my dad would tell me that he was going to leave soon. I left Clark and came home. Five months later while working for Arnold S. my dad died. Seven months later I moved to France with my cat. I had been to Paris for the first time at age 13. I had went on an 11 country tour around Europe. I turned 14 in Italy. I have been to 13 different countries so far.

I spent a lot of time behind the scenes on sets as a kid. Often you might have found me hanging out in Arsenio Hall's green room or hangin out on the set of the old T.V. show Head of the Class. I somehow had become friends with Christine Haag while on the studio lot where mom worked and I would hang out on the set during rehearsals. It's Warner Brother's now but back then it was The Burbank Studios/Columbia Pictures/WB. I love the Warner Brother's lot! I practically grew up on it. Jason Reitman and I would often get into trouble driving carts, sneaking on to closed sets or playing inside the buildings on the back lot.

I have always loved animals and have many great animal stories. The best are the dogs. At age four or five, I was attacked several times by my grandmothers German Shepard, Lion. Normally once would be enough but not for me. I was determined to befriend that dog. I still have scars. At age 12, I was bitten in the face by a dog my mom had got for me from the pound. I had to have plastic surgery to close the two holes in my cheeks as well as my lip which was hanging down to my chin. The doc rocked and no one can tell unless I tell them. Still, I have never feared dogs and have recently worked at a couple of different doggie daycares and I currently work at a dog grooming shop. Oddly enough one of my last boss' was <u>Mike Campbell of Tom Petty and the Heartbreakers.</u> I swear I'm not makin any of this stuff up. He and his wife own one of the doggie daycare's where I used to work.

As far as entertainment, I was a Red Carpet Correspondent at the 2004 SAG awards. I was also a Stand In on Rockstar INXS in 2005. I was also in two Black Eyed Pea's video's back to back in 2005, although you 'll never see me in the video 's. I am an artist, writer, poet, singer, photographer and videographer. I started my own Photo/Video business last year. We specialize in filming and photographing weddings.

I was educated on the East Coast and in France and speak a good amount of French. When I was five I spoke Spanish fluently because my babysitter spoke no English and all the other kids spoke Spanish and watched Spanish T.V. One day the babysitter's 18 year old nephew showed me his penis and that was the end of my Spanish speaking days.

So far, although interesting things happen, I 've been pretty bored with this life, I guess I can say I have been bored since age 3. Ironically I have more interesting things happen in my life than happen in movies. I' ve always been a character. My mom told me that when I was two years old I saw a Mercedes two-seater and said, "Mommy I want that car! That' s my car." My mom said she knew she was in trouble at that point. Not long after that incident my mom had taken me to the Sears in Hollywood. At some point while playing under the clothes racks, I wondered off. Moments after discovering that I had disappeared my mom hears over the P.A. system, "will the lost mother of Alexis Pauling please come to the counter." Of course I couldn' t have been the one who was lost.

I have always been and felt different. I have always been way ahead of my time. I am an ordained minister and I wear a Star of David religiously but I am not religious by any means. I respect religion but personally feel that religion is too confining. I wear the Star because I believe that it is the symbol of balance and creation regardless of religion since it symbolic meaning is: As Above, So Below. I do believe in my heart that I am a descendent of the lost tribes of Israel but I couldn' t tell you much more than that. I also believe that it is because I have remained so open to all possible realities that I have been blessed with such out of this world experiences.

When I first began to awaken I was alone. I had no one to talk to about the wildly amazing thoughts going thru my mind. I did however finally find books which reiterated how I was feeling and thinking. Those books were my best friends during a time of craziness and confusion. I really had to trust myself. I had to trust that I was not crazy even though I was the only person I knew who had swerved off the known path.

While in college, my friend Zoe gave me a book which introduced me to Edgar Cayce. An early twentieth century prophet, who would often go into trance and come up with cures for incurable diseases. Cayce healed many during his life. Thousands of his readings are stored at The A.R.E. in Virginia. Cayce was the beginning. Shortly there after, Zoe gave me another book, 'Many Lives, Many Masters'. The book deals with hypnotherapy and although I had only read half the book, the next day I actually hypnotized Zoe and our other roommate Maddy. I again had absolutely no training but knew I could do it. Zoe went back to age two. She spoke in a baby voice and spoke of being in her grandpa's hospital room eating donuts. When Zoe told her mother of the incident, who by the way doesn't believe in hypnosis, she was shocked and could not understand how Zoe could remember the day with such detail. I had thought that Zoe may have been pulling my leg until, I heard her mother's reaction. When I got back from school I did take a quick course in hypnotherapy. But I felt as if they were trying to hypnotize me into giving them money, so I stopped attending class.

There are many points to these true stories but my reason for sharing them is so that others who do not experience such things will know that magic and the extraordinary do exist. I want us all to look beyond the norm, explore our own as well as others beliefs about reality and keep our minds, hearts and eyes open. You never know what you may experience or see when you are open to all of the possibilities….

MS. Honey Sunshine

Personal Journal of AEHLEX

This is a very strange world. In my heart I know that this planet is very foreign to my soul. I see so many perplexing things & human behaviors that I often wonder if we are in fact in the twilight zone··· 03/19/04

Thanksgiving 1994

Months before my father died I began having very vivid dreams of

my dad telling me that he would be leaving soon. I tried to tell my mom

but she told me not to say things like that so I kept it to myself. My

dad and I spent what I believe was our one and only Thanksgiving

together that year before he died. Within weeks I began having the

dreams. My father passed on May 6th, 1995. He was a very cool guy. He

was instrumental in getting Stevie Wonder started at Motown. My father

was also a great singer, songwriter and record producer. Many of us love

his music but few of us know his name. CLARENCE PAUL. He, his father and

brother Lowman created ···. The Royal Sons quintet. After my father and

grandfather left the group, it became the Five Royales which was the

first ever soul group ···. My uncle Lowman Pauling wrote and first

performed 'this is dedicated to the one I love' . Yes, I come from a

very musical family. Yes, I do sing as well but I sing Rock and Roll.

PARIS

After my dad died I received some money, sent my mom & step dad to Hawaii and in 1996 I went off to live in France for six months with my cat, Kayceo. I had been learning French since age eleven but was still a bit nervous about speaking it at age twenty. I studied at the American University of Paris in France. I lived very close to the Eiffel tower. I lived well in France for four months before I ran out of money. Those last two very broke months were the happiest time of my life. Although 3x more expensive than America it was a lot easier and more pleasant to be poor there. I began to truly understand the physics of life while in Paris. When I had no food I learned that it would come to me. Once while reading my tarot cards I was told that I needed to eat more vitamin C and nuts. Knowing that I did need those things, since it had been a while, I remember wondering where I'd get Vitamin C and nuts with no money. I wondered what I would eat that night but I let it go and didn't think about it. Later that same night I went to the movies with Kim, a friend from school. She had just gotten some unexpected money in the mail and decided to treat me to a movie. The movie was sold out but we did run into one of Kim's friends on our way home as we walked in the rain down the Champs Elyses. He was riding a scooter. We didn't talk much because of the rain. He looked like a sweet kid so I just told him to meet us at my house and gave him directions. Before going home Kim decided to buy us a large pizza. Minutes after we get back to my house Kim's friend arrives with a paper bag. Can you guess what was in the bag? Ironically enough there was a big bottle of orange juice and a big bag of mixed nuts. I'm not lying! I swear! The sweet guy stayed for twenty minutes, never opened the O.J., ate only a few nuts and left the remainder with me. Kim also did not eat much and left the remaining pizza with me. I lived on that stuff for days. Shortly thereafter I got a call and was rescued from financial hell in France by a great friend of mine.

It's a story about having faith. I will try to make it shorter than normal. I had a friend from school take care of my cat while I would vacation in Amsterdam. She often would tell me that I had to meet her friend Faith. Ironically at the same time I had kept telling myself that I had to have faith that Arnold would buy me a plane ticket home, although I refused to ask him. To make a long story short, before going to France, I was working for Arnold. Before an event one day we went shopping . While shopping at J. Crew, a very nice young Lady helped me with the purchase of a suit. Anyway, the day that I came back to get my cat, my friend told me that her and Faith had seen Michael Douglas at a club in Paris. It was the first time my friend had ever been in the same room with a celebrity. She told me that Faith said that the only other time that she had ever been in a room with a celeb was when she had worked at J. Crew, Arnold came into the store with some friends. Faith said she had helped a young lady who was with him buy a suit. I quickly realized that I was the young lady who Faith spoke of. Ironically neither Faith nor my friend (whose name I unfortunately cannot recall) had any clue that the young lady who had bought the suit that day was me until I said, "Oh my God, that was me!" Wow and her name is Faith! I knew that meant that I would be going home soon. Sure enough Arnold called me & asked me if there was anything I needed. He asked me five times in a row before I finally said, "yeah, I'd like a plane ticket home." I never saw Faith while in Paris. We met that one time at J. Crew and then I never saw her again. So far …

Within days of first arriving in Paris, I discovered that I could draw. I had signed up for a drawing class because while working at Arnold's office I became very frustrated that everyone around me had some type of drawing or painting ability. The last straw was when Arnold walked in with an awesome drawing that he had done. I had no idea that he could draw and was flabbergasted. I bought a book about drawing with the opposite side of your brain but I still could not really draw. The first class was very short because our professor only gave us instructions as to what materials we would need and where to find those materials. There was no instruction whatsoever. The next day I went to the art supply store and bought paper, black charcoal and an eraser. Later that night I spoke to Arnold on the phone for the first time since I had arrived in Paris. I told him that I was taking a drawing class. He asked me to send him a drawing. I said ok, then I hung up the phone and freaked out about the idea of having to come up some quality work to show Mr. S. I remember saying to myself… "oh great, I can't draw! What was I thinking? I'm gonna fail this class." I fell asleep stressing about the class. When I awoke I had a very clear image in my mind. I immediately grabbed the paper and charcoal and began drawing. Three hours later the drawing was complete. It looked exactly as it did in my head. I honestly could not believe it. I literally sat on my bed for two hours in shock with my mouth wide open saying, "oh my God! I can draw! Oh my God! I can draw!"

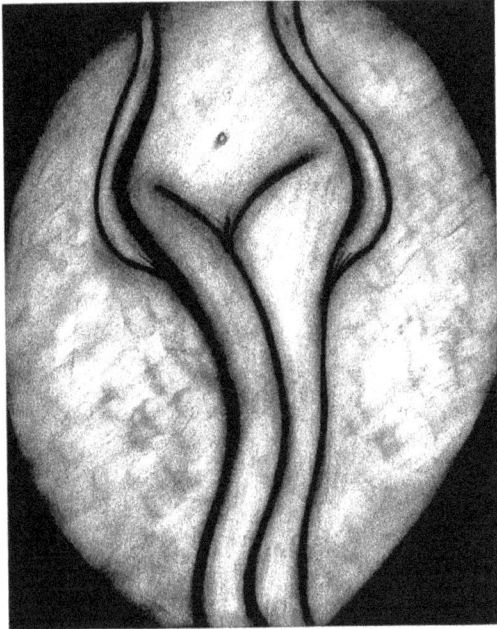

1st Drawing Charcoal Paris France 1996

Robert

Once I got back from France I became acquainted with internet chat rooms. In a room called psychic connections I met a very interesting fellow by the name of Robert S. Robert told me that he had telepathic and telekinetic abilities. I didn't not believe him, but I also didn't know him. One day while chatting on the phone I began to tell him about a strange dream that I had. Before I could finish my sentence he finished describing my own dream to me. He also described what I looked like. Of course I asked him how he knew that and he replied, "I was there". I said, "OK ". We spoke via the telephone and internet for approximately ten days before my cat and I once again boarded a plane, this time to Arkansas to visit Robert. I don't recommend that young girls fly off to meet strangers from the net and I was a little bit concerned but I was willing to risk it. I was supposed to stay two weeks and ended up staying five. I had just turned 21 two months before. I had so many extraordinary experiences while I was there. Here I will only recall a few.

Robert had a pit bull named Thor. Thor was also a Leo and ironically not a lover of cats. So Robert very graciously would leave

Thor outside during the day and Kayceo and I were given the bedroom at night. Very nic,e especially because Robert had a great big waterbed. He also had valium, tons of laser disks, videos, and CD's as well as other tasty treats. So I was in heaven. I have never been a big drinker but I do like to relax. Robert pretty much let me do whatever I wanted and didn't bother me much. He'd take me with him to the store so that I could pick out food that I liked. He is the coolest. He totally took care of me while I stayed at his house and all the while he slept on the couch. A perfect gentleman.

I quickly found out that yes Robert was a very powerful person. He had learned to use his mind in ways most have not even thought to explore. When angered he would sometimes put cracks in the ceiling above him or he would somehow switch on the ceiling fans or other appliances in the house without moving a muscle. One night while sitting together watching T.V., I suddenly had a strange experience. Suddenly the room warped. The entire room warped, The warp effect was like mirage heat waves in the desert. That's the best way to describe it. The room rippled like a heat wave. Stunned I paused frozen for a moment. Then I looked to my right at Robert who I could tell was trying not to laugh. I quickly asked, "did you do that?" He laughed. As I laughed too, I said, "don' t do that!"

Most of Robert' s neighbors seemed to fear him particularly the people directly across the street. When I asked him why he said that he would astral project and visit them in their homes at night. The story that he told of the family across the street was a good one. He said that the twelve year old girl across the street had a crush on him and would always come over and bug him. Not hard to believe. He is a good looking guy. Anyhow, one night he astral projected to the young girls' house, entered her room and began to scream her name. Hearing his voice but not seeing him terrified her but to make matters worse he was grabbing her forearms at the same time so not only could she hear him but she could feel him as well. The girl ran screaming to her mother and after that stopped the annoying random visits to Robert' s house.

I am the type of person who morphs energy. Whenever I am in the presence of someone with a special ability I usually acquire that same ability while in their presence. So while staying with Robert I actually astral projected myself into the past without even trying. It was very strange and very cool all at the same time. I laid on the couch and closed my eyes. Suddenly I am quickly moving thru a tunnel with light and suddenly I was back in my fifteen year old body. I totally remember the day. It was the last day of shooting on the movie Kindergarten Cop. I was sitting in a chair looking at my hands while two friends close by were talking. My hands looked so much different it was strange. Suddenly one of my friends noticed that I was suddenly very interested in my hands and gave me a strange look. At that moment I became nervous and zoom, backward thru the tunnel of lights and back into my 21 year old body. It was interesting to me how quickly fear killed that wonderfully amazing experience.

I also once acquired a Native American friends uncanny ability to know what was about to happen. We had worked on the TV show ER earlier that day and after decided to see a movie. We were standing in line, actually he was standing in line and I was standing against the wall to his left. Suddenly a young man walked up to his mother who was standing in line next to my friend. I looked at the man standing next to me and thought "aren' t you gonna say hi to your friend?" I did not know anything about those three people, so why was I having that thought? The man next to me suddenly looked over at the young man and his mother and said, "hey man, how you doin? Needless to say I was pleasantly surprised by that display of energy.

Robert's dog, Thor ~ 1996

CLAUDIA

Int. Alexis' 3rd floor college apartment Worcester, MA   November 1994

Alexis is sitting in the living room with her roommate Zoe holding the book 'Edgar Cayce the sleeping prophet'

Alexis

Did you know that 98.9 percent of Edgar Cayce's predictions have come true?

Zoe

I know. He has a better record than Nostradamus and not many even know who he is.

Alexis

Well, I am very grateful that you introduced me to Mr. Cayce. He is very enlightening.

His books totally confirm much of what I've been thinking and feeling.

Zoe

What time is your class?

Alexis

In an hour. Oh yeah! Remember how we were talkin' about maybe getting a cat yesterday?

Zoe

Yes⋯

Alexis

Well, I went to the store a few minutes later and there was a lady there with three really cute   little kittens. I was tempted but you weren' t with me and we still haven' t figured out who would   keep it during the holidays.

One hour later while Alexis is standing on the quad lawn before her class, a young hippie chick that she has never seen b4 suddenly walks right up to her.

Hippie chick

Hey man, do you wanna take care of my cat for me?

Alexis looks around for the hidden cameras. Perplexed she responds.

Alexis

Ahh⋯⋯yes actually I was just talkin' to my roommate about that. Weird.

Hippie chick

I' ll take her home during the vacation. I just can' t keep her in the dorm.

Alexis

Oh my God! Yes! That' s perfect!

Hippie Chick

Her name is Claudia. She likes to come outside during the day. If you take her over to the   library during the day, she'll come back to you later if you call her.

Alexis

Oh....kay..very cool

Sure enough after being outside on campus for a few hours, Claudia would always come back to me when I would call her. She also became a model for one of my final photography assignments. She would literally pose for the camera. I swear that cat would not move until she heard the camera click. When I told Zoe about Claudia and her Human friend who I call the hippie chick, Zoe was quite floored as was I. Neither of us had spoken to anyone else about our thoughts on getting a kitty. Neither of us knew the hippie chick **either.**

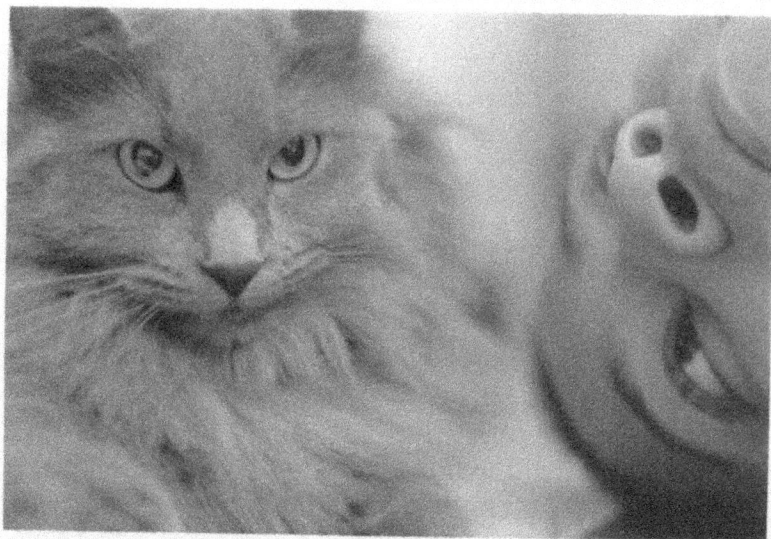

Claudia

Worcester, MA 1994

Poetry by Aehlex…

An urban angle dreams a knock at the door. The knock of consciousness on
issues such as peace and of war. A consciousness so thick, polluted and
maimed, no one loves forever, no one lives without pain.
Lost in the crowd we all look the same.
Where is my voice heard?
Where is my seat on the senate?
No one represents me in the house of representatives.
Ain't no rebellious dredded black chix hangin out in Congress.
I'm smart, I'm beautiful, I'm on the bottom of the totem pole.
Overlooked, unappreciated and worth more than gold.
How much can one stand?
How much will you befriend?
An emotional issue or question.
A ride to the end of the rainbow simply to see the story unfold.
To know the truth, before, during and after you are old.
Give me a cookie cause I've earned my wings.
It may be Winter outside but inside it's Spring.
I sing with the birds in sweet harmony⋯
I can fly! I can fly! Soon I will be,
Soaring and hovering over the trees.
Over the shadows and terrors of night
Over strawberry fields filled with asbestos and mites.
Over heroic danger and drug appetites.
I am complete. I am at peace. I am pleased.
I am lost in the sunshine forever at ease
Giving kisses away to flutterby's and lilies
& for once excepting the fact that it's ok to be silly.

Revolution   12/13/04

It's hard to be excited about this life.
3 jobs a shitty car and still won't eat tonight
Seems like the only thing America offers the poor
Is aggravation, frustration, strife and war!
Overpopulation and under-appreciation of our world
Life is really tragic & scary when you're just a poor American girl.
While homeless children live on our streets
America still claims to be the best & can't be beat

(chorus)
Revolution!
The only solution.
Kill the institution
Their killing the Constitution

I understand poverty and hopelessness
Why say no to drugs when it's the only lift you get?
Can't get ahead no matter what you do
Need money to make money, we're all stuck in a catch 22
We've got to end this cycle of perpetual sadness
Financial instability only creates madness
There's no excuse for unfair slave wages
Unaffordable rents to live in rarely inhabited cages

Revolution!
The only solution.
Kill the institution

Their killing the Constitution

They try to make us afraid to speak the truth
The Patriot act makes me a terrorist too
But I'll never stop. When I do I'll be dead.
You can only push us so far before were pushed over the edge
Soon the revolution will begin once all of our comforts have come to an end!

Revolution!
The only solution.
Kill the institution
Their killing the Constitution

Revolution!
The only solution.
Kill the institution
Their killing the Constitution

By Aehlex

Speakin the Blues

I never know what I'm sayin but you

always seem to have no doubt.

All along thought I was singin

Instead I had to shout!

I never know what I'm sayin but you

seem to have a clue

All the time thought I was singin

Instead I was speakin the blues

Your music gracefully dances in my head.. While the
truth and fear many dread. I walk with passion to the
night and hope to God you won't be right.

_____

This Love

4/18/00

This love is torture but I 'm so addicted to the pain.
This love is torture but I just can't stay away.
I love. I hate. The confusion sucks!
I don't know if you're real but you're close enough.

_____

Is, Ain't

4/25/2000

I always have the light of hope on for you, waiting… waiting...

No more crying for me, I'm all dried up now. All tied up

with rocks of emotion.

Frozen, I've chosen a forgotten path.

Wisdom disintegrates when love is dead.

Everything carousels in me dreds..

I'm crippled with this sadness which instigates my

madness and my anger is ain't the same thing.

I run from direction right into dysfunction and smoke

so much pot I don't dream.

I'm crippled with this sadness which instigates my

madness and my anger is ain't the same thing.

I run from direction right into destruction, then

there's nothing left but pure blame.

All that's left is shame.

All that's left is the pain.

Undue You

6/22/2000

I want to love but anger makes me hate.

I want to love but I've been too raped.

Deep sunshine blues for justice sake...

My God is above worship

Look again at your mistakes like metal in lightening

thunder

Accept the facts reality is change

there's no simple need to wonder

Awake and see, we are all slaves!

The truth will undue you.

I'm not the one you want to blame,

attacking me is futile.. I am here to light the way

attacking me isn't wise.. I am smart and brutal

I can see ahead of my days

to you I just look foolish

I don't care. Go ahead and stare. Gaea loves me, she

keeps me here. For her I have fought many seasons.

Death and Demons ravage our souls and caress us

into volatile reasons. Accept reality! We are all
slaves! The truth does undue you.
I am not the one you want to blame attacking me is
futile. My job is to light the way.. thru the darkness
and forever..directly to our internal knowledge of
buried treasure.

American Sheep

People don't care when children go to prison but get upset when the greedy rich get sentenced. (Martha Stewart)

A woman who shows ONE breast gets a bad reputation, (Janet Jackson)

while the same week a man with a taped molestation gets award recognition (R. Kelly)

Do you want to find freedom or do you think its already here?

Do you want to find freedom or just live in fear?

I'm an American. I have the right to say, "Home of the sheep. Land of the enslaved"

F*CK YOU if you don't like the fact that my country raised me this way!!!!

In this "<u>free</u>" country "<u>liberal</u>" is considered a bad word.

America is now a conservative world.

Conservatives stand against all that America stands for.

They couldn't care less about the homeless, helpless or poor.

They champion causes which stand against peoples rights, all in the name of religion, "morality" and or spite.

When will we take our country back?

When will we get involved?

When will we make "them" respect our votes as more than just a popularity pole?

Reverend Aehlex

The Dogs

I have always had an intense love and curiosity for nature and animals. When about five years old my grandmother's German Shepard, Lion, attacked me several times. As long as I stayed on my bike while in the yard I was fine. I could never stay on that bike. My grandma had Lion's dog house built to look like a miniature version of her house. To me it looked like a play house and I would often try to play in it. Unfortunately every time I would come out of it Lion would be right there waiting to mal me. He busted my head open once. A couple of times I ended up in the hospital. I still have scars on my face to this day from that crazy Dog. Oddly enough I have never been afraid of dogs and German Shepard's are my favorite dogs although I do love all creatures fairly equally.

When I was twelve my mother brought home a dog for me from the pound. A black lhasa apso I named fluffy (nother psychotic dog. About a month after getting the dog there was an incident. My mom had bought something from Ikea and was hammering it together while Fluffy sat in the doorway and watched. Like an idiot I crawled up behind the dog and accidentally scared the crap out of her. She turned around and bit me in the face. My mom started chasing her around the house with a broom as I chase after her pleading, "no. don't kill fluffy. I'm ok!" I hadn't looked in the mirror yet although my mother told me that I'd probably need stitches. I was not in any pain and had not seen my face so I disagreed. The moment I looked in the mirror and saw my face the blood finally started to flow. It was crazy. My bottom lip was torn and hanging to my chin and there were two perfect holes in my cheeks. You could literally see in and out well. Of course I started crying immediately and said, "I'm gonna need stitches." Luckily for me we had insurance at the time and I was stitched up by a plastic surgeon. He was an artist because the scars are virtually undetectable. Thank You! Thank You!

I still never became afraid of dogs. I've had at least fifteen dogs so far. Many of which my mom relocated without my knowledge. I swear mom, they followed me home. Really. I spent two and a half years working at two different doggie daycares in Los Angeles. Often I would work alone with anywhere from twenty to forty dogs. You think I would have learned but no. I would have to break up dog fights alone which isn't always easy. You have about thirty seconds to regain control of the situation before complete pack pandemonium breaks out. You must be very firm, loving and patient because it is important that the dogs trust, respect and love you. You must be the leader of the pact otherwise you are in grave danger. It is so wonderful that these beautiful yet potentially deadly creatures agree to befriend us. I'm sure that they feel the same way about us. Sometimes I did get the occasional accidental bite but it was never a big deal. I do however think that employers and owners of doggie daycares should be required by law to provide health insurance for their employees.

I started this off with a German Shepard and I'll end it with a few. First, Arno, my moms 140 pound pure bred Shepard was one of the most beautiful, smart and awesome dogs ever. He turned lights on and off. He knew how to open any door. He understood as much English as a four year old. Four year olds often speak well. He was funny, playful and protective and a joy to have in our lives.

One night while my mom and step dad were away in India, Arno decided to let me in on a mystery which my mom and I could not figure out. We would leave during the day and when we would get home at night the lights would be on. Mom would half joking, accuse me of doing it and I would blame her but we both knew that it was neither and couldn't figure out what was going on. So this one night while I was watching TV,

Arno decided that he wanted to go outside to the backyard. He had been

out recently so I was not in a hurry to let him out again. My mom

usually does whatever he wants but not me. I told him he had to wait.

Arno complained and sighed continuosly, So I told him that he had to

wait for the commercial to come on. I knew he was just workin me and

hoped he'd go lay down and fall asleep. Once the commercials came on I

thought that maybe if I didn't move, he wouldn't notice but he did. He

got up and walked over to the door. I ignored him so he snapped his big

alligator jaws at me and I just rolled my eyes. I said "No Arno, you

were just out, you gotta wait til I'm ready to let you out again. I'm

not mom!" Then that silly dog went and sat directly in front of the TV.

I maneuvered my head so that I could see around him and he sighed again.

I smiled & said, "what ya gonna do?" He gave me a funny look, got up

walked over to where I was sitting and sat in front of a small table on

the side of the couch near me. There was a gold touch lamp on the table.

Once again I smiled at Arno and asked him, "what ya gonna do, you just

gotta wait?" All of a sudden Arno gave me that funny smirk again and

tapped the light once with his nose and the light got brighter as did my

eyes. Then he tapped the light again and we were sittin in the dark. I

laughed my ass off & then got up & let that crazy damn dog outside. ☺

I immediately called my mom in India and let her know that the mystery had been solved. We both laughed so hard when I gave her the news, because she also reminded me that Arno didn't like being in the dark. Arno died early 2005 and he is greatly missed. He was 10. I'll also mention the Chinese Crested, Gigolo, although we are not on speaking terms. I also must mention that my seventeen year old turtle Mohe also died in 2005. She was a glorious creature. I have had many different creatures. Probably all that are legal. The other really smart German Shepard in my life was Zorro. He was completely jet black. He came here from Hungry and had been trained for the police but was too defensive and not obedient enough for the force so he ended up in America. He lived in a kennel for six months because he would bite everyone who tried to touch him. Finally my step dad brought him home. It took him a year to learn how to play ball. He was very serious in the beginning and very goofy in the end, quite a transformation. He taught Arnie dog tactical maneuvers. He was incredibly well trained and intelligent. I call him super dog because that kid was fierce.

My current animal team is Kayceo the cat (11 years old tuxedo), Sasha Fu (7 years old Shepard Pit mix) and Ms. Honey Sunshine (over 4 years old), she is a dwarf dog. Probably a Corgi /Staffordshire bull

terrier mix. I found her in front of my house while on my way to doggie

daycare. It was funny because the night before I had humorously told my

turtle Mohe, Mr. Fu and Kayceo that I loved them all but they needed to

figure out amongst themselves who was gonna go and get back to me

because somebody had to go. My cat is now on seizure medication twice a

day and turtles are a lot of work. Not to mention Sasha and all of his

antics. I was fed up. I also think that I felt my girl comin because

literally a few hours later I go outside and there she is. I asked her

what she was doing wondering around alone. She followed me to my car and

I put her in. For a second I thought about giving her to my grandmother

or mother but I knew pretty early that I' d probably keep her all to

myself. She was just too cool. I told her that I wanted to call her

something sweet and golden brown because that' s what she was. The first

thing that came to mind was, Taffy. I tried to call her Taffy and I

swear she shook her head and made a sound like a horse nay. I said, "ok

you don' t like Taffy ". A few minutes later I came back and said,

"HONEY! that' s your name!" She quickly responded with licks and

wiggles as if to say, you got it! You finally got it, yes! After work we

went to the vet and then home. This time I told the animals that one of

them needed to get a job. Two months later I had trained Honey enough to get us both booked on FOX's 1ˢᵗ annual Ms. Dog Pageant in 2003. Honey paid the rent that month so I told her she could stay. She wore a sash and I a tuxedo. She was Ms. Conneticut.

The last dog that I will mention here is King. A German Shepard who found us while wondering thru our Hollywood neighborhood. I was about seven. My good friend (brother) Josh and I would take care of King as much as we could. Our parents wouldn't let us keep him in our small apartment so we would keep him in abandoned buildings in the area. Once we put him in our friends dads truck and King broke out the window. He also had ticks. We would burn them off or cut them. I know. Don't cut ticks off of dogs. Well, I know now. Every year my mom would have this friends and family picnic at Griffith park. We always left early in the morning. This year I remember leaving around 7 A.M. Josh and I said goodbye to King and then jumped n the car. Around noon Josh and I see King running up the road toward us. We knew that it was him because he was wearing the bandana/makeshift collar that we had made. He had tracked our scent all the way there. It took him five hours. People told us that they saw him crossing traffic. Shortly after his arrival a man approached us and said, "wow, what a great dog!" Both Josh and I at the same time said "Ya. You want him?" The man said, "yes" and off they went. We didn't say anything about the ticks (we were seven and eight) and we never saw King again. It still breaks my heart but I know that it was right. King came to say goodbye to us and hello to his new life. I'm sorry that we didn't just take you with us buddy. Josh and I were both very protective of our animals so the fact that we were both ok with this guy was a really good sign. If you are out there I'd love to know what happened to our dear friend King. May he rest in peace.

Actual event date: April 30th, 1996

Once while visiting Amsterdam with my college friend Sam, we had a

very strange experience. It was during Queen's Day which is a yearly

celebration of the Queen's birthday. The Dutch love their Queen! A

Dutch friend of mine had earlier told me that everyone from Holland

comes down to Amsterdam to celebrate Queen's Day. Well, he wasn't

kidding. There must have been a million people there that year. On

Queen's Day people sell all kinds of stuff on the street. It's like a

big yard sale. Sam and I were standing at a table looking at various

objects. I was at the end of the table on the left and Sam was to my

right. Suddenly two men walked by me and gave me a bad vibe. They walked

behind us and then stood to the right of us next to Sam. Without a word,

both Sam and I put down what we were looking at, turned to the left and

walked away from the table in perfect unison. As soon as we were far

enough away Sam turned to me and asked, "what the hell was that?" I

replied, "I don't know, just keep movin' those guys were definitely

not cool." When Sam asked "what the hell was that? " he was referring to the feeling that he knew we had both felt. It was literally as if a giant warm hand had moved us away from the two men.

I was not surprised because I know that I am tremendously protected. Sam on the other hand was always tripped out by many of the experiences he would have with me. He started telling everyone that they had to hang out with me because I had mystical energy. I'd always tell him not to say that.

I've had many magical experiences in Amsterdam. The first time I went I was 13. While in college in Paris, France I would take every opportunity to go there. I once spent ten days there alone for spring break. One morning I walked to the Bulldog in the Liedsepliene, sat at a table with two guys that I didn't know from Denmark and shared a joint of super skunk Marijuana with them. Shortly after lighting the joint I see a red-haired man outside wearing jeans and a red bandana on his head and in his back jean pocket. Walking toward the door, he enters and heads right for me. I had never seen him before and no one was around when I bought the bud. At first I thought that he was a redneck until he opened his mouth. He had a thick maybe Dutch accent. He looked right at me and said, "you gotta watch out for the super skunk man, they grow it with chemicals." I looked at him like he was crazy. How could he possibly know what we were smoking and why me? I looked up at him, said, "ok" and then he walked right back out the door and down the street. We all had a good laugh about it and continued smoking. About ten minutes later the three of us were so high that we thought that we were tripping on psychedelics. Totally freaked out the three of us then disperse from the café never to see each other again. Well, I haven't seen them. I also never bought any more Super Skunk, man.

It's a boy!

In my early twenties lived with a family for about a year. The nanny had been trying for a long time to get pregnant. When she finally did get pregnant she believed that she was having a girl but when I would see her or think of her baby, I would often hear a little voice yelling, "I'm a boy, I'm a boy!" However, I kept that voice to myself until one day she passed by me & the little voice was so loud & agitated that I felt compelled to tell. I said, "I know that you think you are having a girl but every time I think about your baby or see you I hear this little voice yelling, "I'm a boy, I'm a boy!" Of course she did not believe me but when the baby was born and the doctor said, "It's a boy!" she later told me that she thought of me immediately. ☺

Jane's Addiction

Jane's Addiction had what they called their 'relapse' tour in 1997. I was a fan, yes, however I must admit that I only knew three of their songs. The three that got most radio play at the time. Jane says, Been Caught Steelin and Mountain song, I believe. I also thought that Dave Navarro was hot and totally bad ass on guitar. Anyway, I had really wanted to go to the concert but by the time I had found out about it, the tickets had been sold out for weeks.

I had been working regularly on Andrew Dice Clay's short lived T.V. show, "Hitz" at Paramount Studios in Hollywood, CA. One Tuesday my co-worker, Adam and I spent the entire day hangin out on set together. It was the same day that Fishbone were the special guests. The cool thing about that show was that every week there were different special guest musicians. I met a lot of people. I ran into Andy Dick again thru that show while hanging out at restaurant Pinot in Hollywood, It was the same day that K.C. and the Sunshine band was on the show. I had met Andy Dick on the set of his movie "Bong Water". I had snuck away during filming to go upstairs and do a quick #2. Yeah, you heard me. Anyway, just as I am washing my hands and right b4 I was able to make a clean break, who else but Andy comes knockin on the door? Busted!

I was so embarrassed and the worst part is that he wouldn't let me walk away. As I tried to leave in shame I said, "sorry about the smell" and Andy said "wait, come here" as he began to pee with the door still open. Anyway to make a long story short, he befriended me then asked me to meet him at The Derby later. I said ok then flaked. The funny thing is that later that week I saw Andy on Hard Copy being snubbed at the door of The Derby. I'm so glad that I flaked. That could have been embarrassing. So, I'd go to restaurant Pinot with a friend who knew one of the "Hitz" producers. Every Tuesday night after the show or shows I should say, the cast and crews would go to Pinot for cocktails and conversation. I met the writers of the MTV show Daria, which was way cool and I also ran into Andy Dick again. I have a funny way of running into Andy in strange places like The Good Guys or that weird, underground Hollywood fetish party that I somehow ended up at. Ahh, good times.. haha! Anyway, I ran into Andy and I told him that these guys from K.C. and the Sunshine band wanted me to go to their hotel later. So Andy and I go there at like 2 in the morning and wake them up from the lobby phone. I just told them to go back to sleep. I felt bad. Wow, I forget how many crazy stories I actually have until I start telling them.

Back to the subject: Late the night before I arrived on the set of Hitz, I was at my friend Shane's house. I remember discussing concerts. I said I wanted to go see Jane's Addiction and Shane said that he wanted to meet Fishbone. So when I showed up on set just hours later and discovered that Fishbone was the special guest I was completely shocked. Adam and I had been hangin out together all day as well as with Fishbone. I must have said that I wanted to go see Jane's a hundred times that day. Earlier that day Adam had told me that he was going to the Jane's Addiction concert that Thursday but it wasn't until later that Tuesday night that he finally told me that he may have an extra ticket. He let me go on all day about how I wanted to go before he told me that there may have been a possibility. Adam called me the next day and told me that the ticket was mine if I wanted it for $20. Needless to say I did not hesitate to say yes. I picked my ticket up just hours before the concert. I was beyond excited!~ 2nd row balcony at The Grand Olympic Auditorium Downtown L.A. I arrived alone wearing a white polyester top with dark blue trim as well as dark blue break dancing sweats with three white stripes down the sides, which I bought the year before while visiting Amsterdam, Holland. As I stood in line waiting to get into the auditorium, a long black limousine pulled up along side of me. The back window came down and I could see Jane's Addiction lead guitarist Dave Navarro. He said hello to a few people in line. I stood frozen. At that moment I thought that Dave was ultra sexy and was shocked that his limo stopped right in front of me. The limo then entered the parking lot and I entered the auditorium. I sat in the 2nd row of the balcony almost in the middle but more to the left of the main stage. As soon as Jane's walked onto stage I tried my best to pay attention to Navarro's every move but my focus kept switching to the lead singer, Perry Farrell. Not only had I never seen him perform but I had never really ever seen him. I had seen some pictures but I had only seen him on TV, MTV once before. I was completely captivated! As strange as it may be, although he did not know me, I remember feeling that Perry had sensed my energy present. He kept looking up in my direction during the show and the strangest thing he didn't do was climb my pillar. That really doesn't sound right without further explanation ☺. Between the main stage and the balcony were two tall pillars. During the concerts, Perry would climb both pillars along with two dancers and then he would proceed to sing to the people in the balcony. As I watched him climb the first pillar I became increasingly excited that soon he would be looking me right in the eyes as he performed because the 2nd pillar was directly in front of me. Perry climbed down the first pillar, walked over to the

2nd pillar then looked up in my direction and completely decided not to climb my pillar. I was so bummed. It was almost as if he felt me there and ran the other way. Regardless, the concert was great! It inspired me to really want to sing and perform.

Perry Farrell

Three weeks after the concert, I got a job at 'The Psychic Eye'
Bookshop in Venice, CA. Every morning I would blast Jane's Addiction as
I vacuumed and prepared to open the store. Three weeks later and six
weeks after the concert, I decided to wear my Amsterdam top to work.
It's the same top that I wore to the concert. Ironically I had not worn
it since and actually very rarely ever wore it. I was at work for about
an hour when suddenly Perry walks in with a tall friend. They walk pass
me, thru the main part of the store to The Annex (the used book part of
the store). They briefly looked around and then walked out the Annex
door. Totally shocked I walked over to The Annex and just stared at my
co-worker Sean. I asked him, "what should I do?" Sean very casually
responded by saying, "go talk to him" . Apparently that's all I needed
to hear because I ran out the door without hesitation. Perry and his
friend were standing in front of the temple next door. I approached
Perry and said, "Wait! You can't leave, you haven't met me yet."
Perry smiled and asked me my name. He introduced his friend as Aaron, at
which point Aaron handed me a flower which he had just picked. Perry and
I chatted for a minute. We talked about how we both didn't like crowds.

Then Perry asked me if I had made it to any of the Jane's Addiction relapse tour concerts. I also noticed that he kept looking at my Amsterdam top, almost as if he recognized it. I told him that I did by some miracle got a ticket for the Olympic Grand show Downtown L.A. six weeks prior to our meeting. I told him I was so excited and amazed by his performance and the band. Perry then asked me if I knew where to find a menorah in the neighborhood. Because my mind was frozen in excitement, I said, "no, I'm sorry" Later I realized that I did know where to find menorah's and I felt like an ass. The funny thing is I never get excited about celebrity's because I have grown up around some of the most influential entertainers in the world. Arnold Schwarzenegger would often say that I am impossible to impress. Well, almost impossible. Although I was somewhat cool and normal when we met, I was completely blown away by Mr. Farrell and that says a lot.

Soon after our meeting, Perry's assistant came into the bookstore and introduced herself to me. I was surprised to discover that her name is Janine and that she is a Capricorn. Why? Because my manager at the bookstore's name is also Jaeneen, although spelled differently, she too is a Capricorn. Janine and I chatted for a moment then she made a purchase and left.

Christmas was near so I decided to buy Perry a wooden Chinese
Dragon. I had planned to give it to Janine the next time I saw her.
After two months of waiting & not wanting to seem weird, all the while
Janine was making frequent visits to the bookstore. And after hearing
Perry's voice in my head very loudly, persistently and repeatedly
singing the lyrics, "you'd better take your chances when you get
them", I decided to finally give Janine the wooden dragon to give to
Perry. Exactly one week later Perry came into the store to thank me. He
also invited me to come down and visit his studio on Abbott Kenney in
Venice. CA. The studio was just a few blocks away from "the eye". I
didn't want to wait too long so I went the next day. Perry gave me a
tour and introduced me to some friends, one of which was Stephen
Perkins, Jane's drummer and one of the best drummers in the world. I
even recited a couple of my cheesy poems for Perry. I wish I hadn't now
but I really just wanted to share back then. Luckily Perry still thought
I was cool and sent Janine down to the store to invite me to a party
that he was having that weekend. Of course I was thrilled! Perry's
parties usually started at 1AM so I would often arrive at 3AM. It was an
interesting time to come into Perry's life. He had conceived his first
child just two weeks prior to our meeting and he was also working on his

sobriety as well as a new form of music, DJing. He was clearing out all the bad things and people from his life. I know in my heart that my energy was needed to help stabilize Perry's energy during this new life transition. My energy is very grounding. I'm not going to go into extreme details about the parties. Although fun, the point of this story is magic and synchronicity. Soooooo many things happened to me in regard to Mr. Farrell I couldn't possibly remember every experience but I will re-count some of the most fun and incredible experiences.

For some still unknown reason, I had a strange telepathic connection to Perry. I remember one night after work as I lay on my bed unwinding, I suddenly heard Perry's voice say, "Alexis, go to St. Marx tonight. I'll be there alone around midnight." I remember thinking, "WHAT? Did I just hear that?" I was tired and annoyed and I didn't want to get out of bed at 10pm to go check out whether or not I was going crazy, but I had to. St. Marx was a club right on the beach in Venice. I arrived at the club just b4 midnight. My friend Benny was workin the door. I stood with my back to the door and chatted with Benny. Suddenly Benny's eyes light up and he says, "hey man how are you?" I turn around and sure enough it's Perry. I looked at my watch and it was exactly midnight. WEIRD! He was alone too which was weird because at this point I had known him for about a year and I had never seen him go anywhere alone. We both seemed kinda wierded out. We spoke for a second. We said hello, how are you? He asked if I was going inside. I said, "no ". He went in and I went home. I had all the info I needed. I still don't know what that was all about.

Another time about a year later, maybe, I had a dream that I had seen Perry at 7-11 with a woman and a kid. . Anyway, I went to 7-11 a couple of hours later and sure enough the moment I pulled up in front of the doors, Perry walked out of the door. He shook his head yes as if he was expecting me. I told him that I knew that I'd see him and that I always knew when I'd see him. Oh yeah and he was there with two woman and a ten year old kid whose b-day they were celebrating. One of the chicas was his girlfriend (I think) but the kid was not his. I didn't really even know what Perry looked like or more than 3 or 4 of Jane's songs b4 the relapse concert. But during the concert and for years after I had many weird things happening around and about this guy. Weird huh?

Around that same time I had been humming the same unknown tune for months. I found it odd but honestly believed that it had to be something that Perry had been working on because I never came up with such cool and detailed melody's. As I said b4 I had some strange connection to Perry. I remember one day not long after first meeting Perry, I began to have strong premonitions about him. One morning I had woken up very depressed and crying. I knew that it was not my feelings and wondered how Perry was feeling as strange as that may sound. Well three days later, Perry came by the store. It was raining out. We stood outside. As I twirled around and danced in the rain, Perry told me that he liked cloudy days. He also told me that he had woken up three days ago really depressed. I was so siked that he told me that because of course I would not have asked nor did I tell him of my experience. I'm sure he would have questioned my sanity so I kept it to myself although I was dying to tell him all of this crazy stuff that kept happening. Anyway, on Sunday nights at St. Marx, Perry would often spin. I was upstairs one night with his friends in the VIP loft sitting at a table with a couple of folks. Perry started to play a new song from his (at the time) soon to be released solo album. As soon as I heard it I freaked out and exclaimed, "Oh my God! That's it! That's the song I've been humming. I knew it had to be Perry!" The song was Happy Birthday Jubilee. Of course everyone looked at me as if I was nuts but I didn't care. I knew what was up. I get the crazy thing a lot but it doesn't bother me. I know who I am and I also know how blind most people are to true reality which is very enchanting and magical. So I don' t care much about what others think. Although I do like telling my stories and want my readers to know that they are all true.

Another strange thing that happened occurred about six months into knowing Perry. I was hanging out with some people in Perry' s crew. One of his friends was telling another friend where Perry lived. Oddly enough I remember covering my ears and humming because I didn' t want to know. I figured that if Perry wanted me to know where he lived, he' d tell me. Not too long after this incident, a (girl) friend of mine named Charlie and I were looking for places to live in Venice. Charlie was driving and I was in the passenger seat. We passed the address we were looking for so Charlie made a U turn. As she turned I suddenly spotted Perry' s car as well as Aaron' s parked in front of a very unusual house which I will not describe because he may still live there. I knew right away that it was Perry' s house and later confirmed that fact. I guess the universe felt I should know his address for whatever reason.

These are just a fraction of the strange occurrences which I experienced for years after meeting Perry. His music also playfully haunted me. While listening to CD' s or even the radio, Perry' s music would often be in sync w/ my thoughts and actions. This is tuff to explain but I'll give you an example: One day while trying to explain all of this to my roommate Myra, I decided to put on a Porno for Pyro's song called Bloody Rag because I wanted her to hear the drums in the song. As we listened to the song I told her some of the weird synchronistic things that were happening in regards to Perry. Myra had a hammock in her room. I tried to sit in it and fell onto the floor. Myra laughed of course and said, "Ah huh, Ah huh" because I was being silly when I fell. As soon as she said that, Perry repeated the same exact words in the song, "Ah huh Ah huh". Myra almost fell over in shock. Remember she had NEVER heard the song before. She just sat there with her mouth open and all I could say was, "That's exactly what I'm talking about! Why is this stuff happening to me?"

The last time that I saw Perry, I knew it was gonna be the last time, at least for a long time. Before I left Perry had bought us all bagels. As I was leaving Perry asked me if I was taken off. I said yes and then Perry looked me in the eyes and grabbed and squeezed my hand. I left the studio that morning, sat in my car and cried for a few minutes before I left. That's how I knew I wouldn't see him for a while. I don't ever cry for no reason. I really like Perry. Although a bit quirky, he's fun and somewhat magical. I am very glad that I was fortunate enough to spend anytime with him let alone a good year of my life. I saw Perry again at a fashion show three or four years later. He was with his new wife. We greeted each other briefly and that was it.

The So-called shape shifter

Ok here is one more story. This also happened while I was working

at the psychic eye in Venice. One Sunday we had a staff meeting. As a

rule I try not to work on Sundays although there was a time that I would

work in the Annex every Sunday. The Annex was the used part of the

bookstore. This particular Sunday I was not working, only attending the

staff meeting. The meeting ended shortly b4 the store opened at 11am. A

few minutes later I went to open the door and then I was going to leave.

As soon as I got to the door I saw a man outside whom I had seen a

couple times b4. I had not had any encounters with him other than looks

but I did suspect that in him was a demon whom I had met b4. This entity

would body hop from schizophrenic to schizophrenic. He would always come

into the store and do the same exact thing in different bodies. He would

come in look at me with the same facial expressions on each different

face. Walk over to this book with Jesus on the cover. Then it would look

at the book, look at me and then look at itself in the mirror, over and

over again. I began to recognize its energy very quickly regardless of

the fact that it would appear in different form. Right away I told

Strider, who was at the time working with me at the psychic eye, to watch him and that he was a shape shifter. He/it is not a shape shifter but I needed to explain fast and I knew that Stridee would know what I meant. Actually I said, "Strider, there's this guy walkin around outside. As soon as I open this door I know he's comin in here. He's a shape shifter and he likes to fuck with me. So watch him cause I'm leavin'. Normally I didn't watch the customers too closely because many who stole from "the eye" would bring the items back apologetically so I figured that was between them and karma. But something told me to follow this guy. He walked into the Annex where no one else was, picked up something while mumbling and then placed it into his pocket. I was standing in the doorway watching. I told him that I'd have to ask him to take that out of his pocket and then I'd have to ask him to leave. He tried to pretend that he didn't know what I was talkin about then finally took a card out of his pocket placed it on the table and started yelling at me, "Jesus was a murderer!" I handed him off to Strider and the so called shape shifter started yelling at Strider, "I am Ezekiel!"

I walked over to the table to see what he had tried to steal. It was a Jesus prayer card, weird for a guy who didn't like Jesus. Why he was yellin at me about Jesus I don't know. OK, I do know but I'm not tellin. All I know is that there were 3 candles on the table against the wall of saints (a wall full of plaques of Saints and many of Jesus). One white candle in the middle of the table and two red candles, one on both sides of the white candle. The white candle's holder was about two or three inches taller than the two red candle's holders. Also the candlestick holders which the red candles were in were brand new. To make a long story short, the guy was standing in front of the candles b4 I threw him out of the store. When I went back I found the prayer card and also the two red candles bent like boomerangs. I had closed the Annex the night b4 and had looked at the details on the new holders b4 leaving and locking up. I took the candles around to see what everyone would say. Most thought that they had melted. Finally Strider chimed in and said, "look people if it's not hot enough during the day to melt candles how could it be hot enough at night when the sun's not out?" I said, "Thank you!" As I was putting them back to try and get a few customer reactions, the assistant manager came over and said excitedly," you didn't tell me they came from here. I was just checking these candle stick holders out this morning because they are new. Those candles were not like that an hour ago." Then I said, "I know! I was in here this morning and last night. The only other entity in this room today was that creepy demon. I know that he bent these candles telekinetically."

I took the candles into the manager's office while she was outside smoking. She was also my best friend so I could get away with swiping her keys when she wasn't lookin. Knowing that no one else would go into her office, I figured that would be a great place to stash the candles. I was a bit nervous about taking them home. I snuck into the office when no one was lookin. Climbed up the 8 ft bookcase and put the candles on top of a dust pile. No one had been up there in years if ever. No one saw me go in or out yet three days later when I went back for the candles they were gone. I questioned everyone and NO ONE knew what had happened to those candles. I must say I totally believe them all. The candles simply vanished or I should say were taken by something but not by anyone.

INTERIOR ~ THE MYSTIC EYE BOOKSTORE ~ MAIN SIDE ~ SAME MORNING

Two customers walk in.

Jonahs is sitting on a stool behind the main counter.

                              AEHLEX

          Where did Jeanette go?

                              JONAHS

          I think she's outside smoking. Man, you weren't

          kidding about this place.

                              AEHLEX

          No, I wasn't . I guess that was your initiation. I'll

          be right back. Can you please stay here and answer

          the phone if it rings? Let me know if someone

          wants to buy something, I'll be right outside. Aight.

                              JONAHS

          Alright.

EXT ~ OUTSIDE IN FRONT OF THE MYSTIC EYE BOOKSTORE ~ SAME MORNING

Aehlex walks outside and finds Jeanette and Ron smoking.

                    RON
          (to Aehlex)
     Jeanette was just telling me about your friends job

     over at Alien Archives. That's all just a load of crap.

                    AEHLEX
     What is?

                    RON
     Aliens.

                    AEHLEX
     Oh really?

                    RON
     Yeah, really.

                    JEANETTE
     Oh no.

                    AEHLEX

Ok. Can I ask you something then?

RON

Sure go ahead.

AEHLEX

Where are we?

RON

What do you mean where are we?

AEHLEX

What, am I not speaking English? I mean exactly
what I said. Where are we?

RON

(sarcastically)

Uhhh Venice.

AEHLEX

Um humm. And where's that?

RON

Where are you going with this?

AEHLEX

Come on just humor me, please.

RON

Ok. Um Los Angeles.

AEHLEX

Good. And where's Los Angeles?

RON

In California.

AEHLEX

Where's California?

RON

In the United States.

AEHLEX

Where's the U.S.?

RON

Planet Earth and the Earth is in the Milky Way

galaxy, ok. Are we done?

AEHLEX

Not quite. Where's the Milky Way?

Ron just sits quietly for a moment, thinking.

> RON

The Milky Way is... within our solar system.

> AEHLEX

Uh huh. And where is our solar system.

> RON

(pause) In this Universe.

> AEHLEX

Yeah, but where in this universe? And, where is this universe?

> RON

(aggravated)

I don't know!

> AEHLEX

My point exactly. You don't even know where you are, yet you are convinced that we are the only life around. We can't even get around most of our own solar system more the less explore beyond it and you're going to stand there and tell me that there is no doubt in your mind whatsoever that we are the only "so-called" intelligent life in an infinite universe. Oh please, wake up! That's just purely ridiculous and incredibly arrogant!

RON

Whatever.

AEHLEX

You're probably also one of those people who thinks that the Earth has no consciousness or emotion. Huh? You probably think that she's just one big round house for all of us and has no other purpose. Don't ya?

RON

Please, tell me, what is her other purpose?

Aehlex shakes her head no and laughs.

AEHLEX

You're such an idiot. That would be like the tiny cells in our bodies laughing at the notion that we are conscious feeling beings with functions other than to simply just house them. Do you see what I'm saying?

RON

(agitated)

You're crazy!

Ron goes back inside the bookstore.

AEHLEX

Yeah sure, I'm the crazy one.

Aehlex sits down next to Jeanette.

JEANETTE

(to Aehlex)

You two.

AEHLEX

Why did Marty hire that kid? He's so clueless.

JEANETTE

I don't know.

AEHLEX

I do have fun messin with his head though. It breaks

up the day.

Jeanette just shakes her head puts out her cigarette and stands up.

JEANETTE

(laughs)

You ain't right.

Aehlex also stands up.

AEHLEX

(laughs)

Maybe not. But I'm also not often ever wrong either.

INTERIOR ~ THE MYSTIC EYE BOOKSTORE ~ MAIN SIDE ~ SAME MORNING

Aehlex and Jeanette both walk back inside the bookstore.

Ron is in the back of the bookstore.

Jonahs is still sitting behind the counter but now is sitting on the chair instead of the stool.

Aehlex goes behind the counter and sits on the stool in front of the cash register.

MUSIC: 'By your side' from Sade's Lover's Rock album .

JEANETTE

I'll be in my office if you need me.

Jeanette walks away.

AEHLEX

(to Jeanette)

Ok.

(yells)

Hey Ron. Come here,

RON

(yells back with attitude)

What?

AEHLEX

(to Ron)

I want to tell you a story so you don't think I'm so crazy.

(to Jonahs)

Or maybe it will just make you think that I'm even

more crazy. I don't know.

(to Ron)

Will you come here, please?

Ron walks over to the main counter and just stares at Aehlex.

AEHLEX

First of all, I'm sorry I called you an idiot. That

wasn't very nice and I apologize.

                    RON

Thank you. I'm sorry I called you crazy.

                   AEHLEX

   (smiles)

That's ok. I'm used to it.

                    RON

So what's your story?

Kevin and Gaea

                   AEHLEX

Alright. I was working on this TV show a couple of

months ago and this guy Kevin and I decided to walk

over to this mini mall next door during one of our

breaks. So anyway, on our way back:

FLASH BACK

EXT ~ MINI MALL NEAR MANHATTAN BEACH STUDIOS ~ MANHATTAN BEACH,

CA ~ CLOUDY DAY

Kevin is about 6'3" ~ African - American, part time fire-fighter. He is wearing a long black leather coat.

Kevin and Aehlex walk out of a liquor store and underneath a large awning.

Suddenly it begins to hail.

KEVIN

Oh man, my coats gonna get ruined.

AEHLEX

No it won't. All we have to do is ask Gaea , I call

the Earth, Gaea. All we have to do is ask her to

stop the hail by the time we get out from underneath

this awning. Watch.

Kevin looks at Aehlex like she's crazy.

KEVIN

Man, I just bought this coat.

AEHLEX

(looks up)

Gaea can you please stop the hail once we are on

the side walk?

The moment before they hit the sidewalk the hail abruptly stops.

Kevin just looks at Aehlex.

                         AEHLEX
                 (to Kevin)
             Told ya.
                 (looks up)
             Thanx Gaea.

They walk back onto the studio lot.

EXTERIOR ~ MANHATTAN BEACH STUDIOS PARKING STRUCTURE ~

MANHATTAN BEACH, CA ~ CLOUDY DAY

As soon as Kevin and Aehlex enter the ground floor of the parking structure, it begins to drizzle.

KEVIN

Great! Now it's drizzling.

AEHLEX

Oh she's just messing with us. As soon as we get

out it will stop.

They leave the shelter of the parking structure and the drizzling stops.

AEHLEX

See. Watch this. Gaea can you please make it drizzle

lightly right now?

It begins to drizzle lightly.

Kevin is silent and shocked.

AEHLEX

Thank you. Ok can you please stop.

The drizzle stops.

Aehlex looks over at Kevin and smiles.

> **KEVIN**
>
> What???

> **AEHLEX**
>
> Thank you. Can you please drizzle lightly for me one
> more time.

It begins to drizzle lightly again.

> **KEVIN**
>
> This is crazy!

> **AEHLEX**
>
> Ok, Gaea please stop drizzling now, we don't want to
> ruin this nice young man's new coat.

The drizzle stops.

> **AEHLEX**
>
> Thank you. See, all you have to do is communicate
> with and respect the Earth and she will respond kindly.

FLASH BACK ENDS

INT ~ THE MYSTIC EYE BOOKSTORE ~ MAIN SIDE~ SAME DAY

MUSIC: Sade's Lover's Rock album plays softly throughout scene.

RON

Is that story true?

AEHLEX

No. I just made it up to impress you. Of course, it's a
true story. I've got a pretty decent imagination but it
ain't that great. I was actually telling two guys this story
one day while filming the movie K-Pax at the train station
Downtown L.A. The two guys were just looking at me as if
I were crazy when suddenly just as soon as I finished telling
the story, who walks by holding a wardrobe bag? Kevin,
of course. Well, I had not seen him since the incident. I
exclaimed, "oh my God! I was just telling them the story
about the hail and rain the day we met at Manhattan Beach
Studio's. I've been wanting to run into you because I was
wondering if I could have permission to use your name in
the book that I am writing" Kevin said, "Yeah, that shit was crazy!"
then he gave me permission to use his name and kept walking.
Later, after we wrapped, I was standing in the parking lot with
the two young men that I was telling the story to earlier. As we
chatted it began to rain. The car I had at the time was very unsafe
in the rain. I told the guys that Gaea (The Earth) didn't really rain

much when I would have to drive. I looked up to the sky and asked

her to stop by the time I was ready to leave. We continued to

speak for a few minutes and just as our conversation wrapped up,

the rain became lighter and lighter. I said goodbye to the two guys and

told them that it would take me about ten minutes to get home, & that

it probably wouldn't start raining again until then. As soon as I got into

my car the rain stopped. It did not begin again until I arrived home

ten minutes later. I always wonder if those two guys noticed.

Ron just shakes his head and walks away.

Aehlex notices that there is a large green gem with a metal necklace fitting on the top, sitting on the desk next to the large appointment book. She walks over and picks it up.

AEHLEX

What's this doing out here?

Sunrise walks over to the counter and picks up the large appointment book to see if she has any appointments.

Sunrise is one of the Mystic Eye psychics. She is young & Caucasian & dresses between a hippie and a gypsy.

SUNRISE

Alexis, can you check and see if there is any money

in the cash register for me?

AEHLEX

Sure.

Aehlex puts the green jewel back down on the desk and walks over to the cash register and opens it up. She lifts up the cash drawer.

AEHLEX

Nope, sorry.

Sunrise finishes looking at the book she drops the appointment book on top of the green jewel.

Both Sunrise and Aehlex hear the jewel fly off the table.

SUNRISE

Oh, what was that?

AEHLEX

Probably that green piece of jewelry that I just put
down there.

Aehlex lifts up the appointment book and begins searching every square inch behind the counter.

Sunrise comes over to help look.

They search everywhere. In the trash bin, behind and underneath things. But the jewel is no where to be found.

                              AEHLEX

              Where the hell did that thing go? It's weird that we

              can't find it.

                              SUNRISE

              I'm so sorry.

                              AEHLEX

              Don't worry about it. I'm sure it will turn up.

A customer walks in.

Sunrise goes back to her room.

                             CUSTOMER

                  (to Aehlex)

              Could you show me where I can find the family

              of light books.

                              AEHLEX

              Sure can. Follow me.

Aehlex walks the man over to the book tables where many best selling books are laying flat.

                              AEHLEX

              Here you go. Bringers of the dawn, Earth and The

              Family of light. We don't have the new one yet but

it should be here soon.

CUSTOMER

Thank you very much. I like your Star of David.

Are you Jewish?

AEHLEX

(abruptly)

I believe I am a descendant of the Lost Tribes of

Israel. If there's anything else I can help you with

just let me know.

CUSTOMER

Ok. Thanx again.

Aehlex walks back behind the counter and sits down in the chair at the desk.

Jonahs walks back in and sits on the stool by the cash register behind the counter.

AEHLEX

That was a quick break.

JONAHS

I just needed some fresh air.

There is a box of Palladini tarot cards in front of Aehlex to her left.

                              AEHLEX

              I'm bored. I'm gonna give myself a tarot card reading.

              Do you ever read the tarot?

                              JONAHS

              Yeah. I like the Aliester Crowley deck..

                              AEHLEX

              That's a cool deck but it's a little too dark for me.

              I use the new Palladini deck. It's very similar to

              the Raider-Waite deck except it has better pictures

              and colors.

Jonahs is looking at Aehlex.

Aehlex puts her left hand on the tarot card box. At the exact same moment the green jewel shoots
out of a dark corner behind the box at an angle.

SFX: There is a sound of swiftness as the jewel fly's thru the air.

Aehlex's head quickly turns to look at her right hand which is now level to her head, in the air
and closed. She has caught the jewel without even looking or trying.

JONAHS

(shocked)

What the fuck was that?!!!

Aehlex opens her hand.

AEHLEX

That I believe, was Bobby. But I'll tell you all about

him another time. Thank God I have such great reflexes.

Are you ready to quit yet?

JONAHS

Not yet.

Aehlex grabs a set of keys and locks the green jewel in the jewelry case.

It's an integral part of being.

While living in Palms, California sometime during 1995, I began my
UFO education. I was taught how to spot them in the sky. I was taught to
differentiate between them and stars, satellites, planets and planes.
They simulate these things so that it is easier to drift thru our skies.

I was living alone although my cat, Cayce (Kayceo) did come to
live with me that year. I began to notice that a certain star would
appear and disappear at the same times each night while the other stars
would remain still. This one particular star also did things that the
others never did. It shot out little orange lights and hovered. It also
communicated with other red lights in the sky. I assume that these were
smaller related vessels. I didn't know much about UFO's at the time
but I did have a firm belief in the probability of their existence. I
was 18.

I remember watching them while outside on my balcony. One night I
asked, "what do you want from us? Why can't you just leave us alone?"
That's very funny to me now. Anyway I turned around to go inside after
asking the strange star that question and before I could get both feet
in the door I heard a loud male voice in my head say, "it's an
integral part of being." I repeated what I had just heard a couple of

times aloud. I ran to the dictionary to look up the word integral because I didn't know what it meant. It means necessity for completeness. Thank you but the last thing I expected to receive was a response. From that point on I trusted that the strange stars were not stars at all.

In 1998 I channeled for the first time in my life. I was now living in Venice, CA. I was on my way out the door of my friend Strider's house when suddenly some dear old friends began to chime in. I call them the Intergalactic Federation of Light. Beings of light and love from all over this universe and beyond whose job is to help maintain order without interfering very much or at all. This meeting had been pre-planned and was not in any way an intrusion into my reality. I expected it and welcomed them. They were very excited and speaking over each other. I became flustered and asked that they speak one at a time. Strider asked questions. He asked when they would be coming to see us. We felt that we needed to see them because although we believed and knew that they were real, we also knew that our logical minds would need more proof before being able to truly accept the reality of their being without doubt or question. Strider offered to meet them in the desert. I rejected that proposal since the ocean was much closer. One of the entities said, "Ok see you soon. One month by the lagoon." Three weeks later I asked Strider "the Virgo" if it had yet been a month and he snapped gruffly, "no, it's only been three weeks!" The following Friday (sometime I think in November of 1998) my friend and co-worker Charlie, led Strider and I up the side of this hill just past Topanga Canyon over PCH. Charlie also brought two dogs. Egypt and I could never remember that other dogs name. Charlie was not too aware of UFO's but she was open to it. Strider was working at UFO central in Venice at the time and I was working at the Psychic Eye as was Charlie.

As soon as the sun went down I spotted the first one. As usual Strider proceeded to argue with me about it. He tried to tell me that it was just a star. He put his hand up as if to measure it against the other stars in the sky and at that very moment all the stars over our heads fell out of the sky and disappeared. That tripped me out because I really had thought that those were all stars. Then in my head I hear someone say, "that was the first of 80 ". After that we saw so many different types of craft. It was really awesome. There was telepathic communication going on throughout the experience. We had sat and watched the flight paths for a while before the sun went down so we new that these craft were not on the flight paths. We saw what looked like the mother of the stealth bomber. We also saw a large craft that looked exactly like a rocket ship except that it flew side-ways like an airplane. We saw one really large round ship with lights all around it. We saw one very odd craft. It looked like one of those 4th of July sparklers. It was long and skinny stick like craft which had big bright sparklers at each end. I have seen a similar effect on planes but those sparklers flash these did not. So many craft. There were also orbs, little robotic spies. The list goes on and on. I can hardly remember all the different types of craft that we saw. At one point we were sitting me in the middle, Strider at my left and Charlie at my right. We were all looking in different directions while trying to get the others attention. This seemed to go on for hours. Strider says that it was about two hours although I felt like we were out there for six. At some point Strider walked away into the darkness. He was gone for about ten minutes before I began to worry about him and yell his name. Suddenly Charlie, the dogs and I hear footsteps. I yell out, "Strider, is that you? " No response. "Strider? "

Suddenly the figure coming toward us came into view. It looked as if the mountain was coming toward us. The dogs growled. Charlie and I confirmed that we were both seeing the same thing. The closer the figure got the clearer it became. Strider who was wearing a tan poncho, looked as if he had camouflaged with the natural surroundings and the mountain. He smiled deviously. I said sarcastically, "why didn' t you answer me? You shit, you scared us. You totally morphed with the mountain it was crazy it looked like the mountain was walking toward us. " Close to the end of the night I realized that some of our friends were probably around us and yet undetectable to our eyes. Soon after that realization we began to see what I call the invisible people. I say invisible because you could only see the outlines of people It is difficult to explain. We began wandering around the mountain that we were on. We began to notice that certain spots were much warmer than others. We could walk in and out of these warm spots or stand half in and half out. It was strange. After a while the warm spot would get cold and we would move until we found another one. We did that a few times before we left.

The last event of the evening was when I was told telepathically that someone was waiting to meet us at the top of this hill. I lead our group to the hill and began walking up it. I had not given Charlie or Strider any explanation for why we were walking up the side of a mountain without a path but they gladly followed none the less. About a quarter of the way up I decided not to continue. I stopped and turned around. At that moment Strider Screamed, "Damn it!!!" I jumped and said, "what?!" Then he said, "They just told me that it was up to you if we would go and you stopped and turned around." I just smiled and apologized. I wasn't in the mood for poison Ivy and mountain climbing besides we had a great night and I wasn't sure if we were already overloaded on the experience. So I just decided to take a rain check with our friends. I'd like to take this moment to thank them. Thanx….

By the way, Strider went back to work at UFO central that Monday. He and his co-workers received many strange activity in the sky reports from people in the Topanga/ Malibu area.

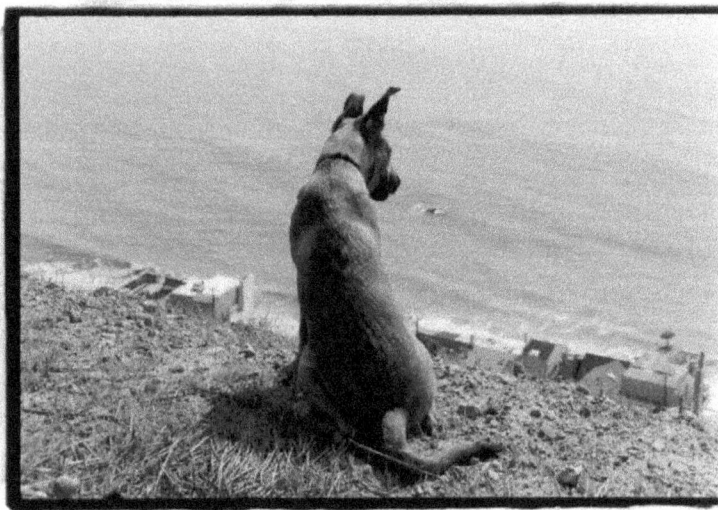

Mr. Sasha Fu sitting over PCH in the spot where we saw the many UFO's

The woman with no white around her eyes....

About one month or so after the UFO sightings over PCH

(approximately December 98' or January 1999) I had an encounter with

a woman from another world. I was working at the Psychic Eye Bookshop

at the time. It was probably a Sunday because I liked to work in the

annex on Sunday's. The annex was the used section of the bookstore. I

was standing behind the counter at the register as was Strider and Paul.

Strider was to my right and Paul was to his right. Paul was always

skeptical about our sightings. Three years after this incident, it occurred

to me that I could have totally gotten fired for allowing the guys back

behind the counter. It was not something I normally would allow but in

hind sight the only way the fellas would have been able to see what was

about to take place. Suddenly a very tall, thin, Caucasian woman came

around the corner from the main side of the store. I knew that she was

headed right for me. She was bald, wearing sunglasses, a white wife

beater, khaki shorts and sandals. She was also holding a stack of flyers.

As she began to speak to me she took off her glasses. Strider and Paul for

once were silent. She asked me if she could put her flyer up on our

bulletin board. I, always surprised at how calm I can be in extraordinary

situations, casually responded by saying, "no, I'm sorry that is only for

our psychics. People ask all the time." She said thank you. Put on her sunglasses and left. Paul started talking as if he hadn't just seen what we know he did so Strider and I at the same exact time said "woe woe woe back it up". It took Paul a couple years to admit to me that there was something very odd about the tall lady. Strider and I spoke about where she may have been from. Why? Because although her eyes were shaped like a human's, they were anything but. As a matter of fact they looked like the eyes of a Grey alien. Where we have pink her eyes were charcoal Grey. There was no white around her eyes either. They were a filmy black color with a slimy looking texture. Definitely not Hollywood makeup. I grew up around the biggest special effects guy in Hollywood and this was not his work. Unfortunately we never got a look at the flyer because we were too busy being mesmerized by her eyes.

About an hour later I was sitting outside taking a break when I spot that woman walking with a man and a tiny Chihuahua. They were walking down Main Street in Venice toward Rose Ave. I was across the Street thinking about how odd they appeared. They were both wearing identical outfits and they were like carbon copies of each other. Both the exact same height and build. Both bald. The only difference was that you could tell one was female because she had breasts. They appeared to be acting as if they were boyfriend and girlfriend but once I realized that we didn't have male and female identical twins on this planet I knew that they were alien. I immediately began speaking to them telepathically.

Without a word, I said, " I know that you can hear me. I know that you can read my thoughts." At that very moment they both stopped and turned and looked at me in unison. I said, "thank you. Thank you very much." and they walked away.

One week after that while sitting in my car at lunch with Jaeneen the store manager, I had another encounter. Jaeneen and I would often sit in my car (Ethel May) during lunch. We rarely ever spoke or listened to music. We were just so happy to be away from the madness of the bookstore that we would just sit in silence. This day we were parked in front of the ocean exactly two blocks away from "the eye". I am a very security minded person who is always looking around and in my mirrors even while at a standstill. I had just did my momentary security sweep of the situation and there were no humans to be found in any direction. I had looked around, I looked in both my side mirrors and then finally my rear view. The moment that my eyes shifted away from the rear view mirror two car doors slammed. The tall woman, her identical male twin & the tiny Chihuahua dog all got out of the green car behind us. The woman walked by my side in the street and gave me a glance. The man and the dog walked around the passenger side & down the sidewalk. Perplexed I asked Jaeneen if she had heard the car doors open. She said, "no" & I said, "neither did I." A silly question because they literally had no time to get to the car, get in & then get out between the time I had

looked away from the mirror & heard the car doors slam. Then I asked.
"Do you remember me telling you about those people from earlier this week?" Jaeneen said, "yes" Then I said, "that's them" Jaeneen just said "nooo" nervously. Then she asked, "What do you think they want?" I said, "I don't know. I think they want to talk to me but either they aren't ready to talk to me or they don't think I'm ready to talk to them. Either way as long as they keep walkin we'll be alright." And they did. I haven't seen them since. That was probably January of 1999. Shortly thereafter I had had enough & quit that crazy job. I just couldn't take anymore. There were so many strange occurrences at that place. One time a guy actually accused me of swelling up his feet. I'm not makin this stuff up. I promise. I'm not that creative. Trust me. He said, "I came into this store the other day & you walked by me wearing that Star of David & now my feet are swollen."

Abstract Realism ~ The Movie

The following are excerpts from a script that I wrote of many of my

adventures. I did change some names. For instance Joseph represents

Strider. I did change the names back at the end for the Topanga Canyon

UFO story which I have already written about earlier in this book. Some

stories will be repeated in this script but with more detail. The script

is 97% true. All of the writings (other than these script excerpts which

are 97% true) are 100% true. In the script some stories and characters

have been combined and a few scenes have been created in order to fit

true stories into the scenes and script. These script excerpts will give

you more insight into my world.

FADE IN FROM BLACK

MUSIC: Led Zeppelin's 'Whole Lotta Love ' has begun playing.

OPENING CREDITS OVER A MONTAGE of skateboarders on a pipe, the ocean and sites around Venice, California that are on the way to Aehlex's house not far from the ocean. The camera travels basically from the beach to Aehlex's front door. Then the shot continues on the opposite side of the front door inside the house but still on the door. The shot opens up to things in Aehlex's house, like her turtle and snake and bullfrog, her tarot cards, books (Seth Speaks and The Nature of Personal Reality by Jane Roberts, Edgar Cayce, Green Eggs & Ham by Dr. Seuss) her art work, & CD's which are on a <u>WALL POSTER CD RACK</u> (Nirvana, Jane's Addiction, Green Day, Smashing Pumpkins, Sublime, The Doors, Mahalia Jackson, Clarence Paul, The Five Royals, Stevie Wonder, Marvin Gaye, Royal Trux.) She also has a bright yellow and orange poster that says "Fiat Lux" (let there be light). About one minute and 15 seconds into 'Whole Lotta Love' we enter Aehlex's bedroom.

INT - AEHLEX'S BEDROOM - MORNING

AEHLEX (Alexis) is in her 20's, a beautiful African American female who looks a lot like Lisa Bonet with dreadlocks. And she always wears a **Silver Star of David** around her neck. She is extremely liberal and lives alone in a small one bedroom house in Venice, CA with her two dogs, cat and reptiles. She is just waking up. She rolls over, opens one eye and sees something strange on her night stand. Once both her eyes fully open, she can see that it's a baby bird claw.

106

Music fades…

AEHLEX

(surprised)

Ahhhh… Kayceo! Damn it! No presents!

(mumbles)

Damn cat!

She gets out of bed & scoops the bird's claw into the trash with an index card.

AEHLEX

Thank You. I truly appreciate the thought but it's

ok, really. I know how much you love me. There's

no need to give me presents. Geez….

Aehlex's dog, HONEY (a 3 year old female Corgi/ Stafford-Shire Terrier mix with short dwarf

like legs, a big head, long muscular honey colored body and turned in ballerina front legs), peeks

her head around the corner.

INT- LIVING ROOM - MORNING

Aehlex walks from her bedroom into the living room followed by Honey.

                    AEHLEX

        Good morning, Honey. Have you seen Kayceo?

        I'm gonna kill that crazy cat if she doesn't stop

        Bringing me dead presents.

        (pause)

        And where's Mr. Fu?

Aehlex turns on the T.V. The news comes on.

                NEWS ANCHOR (V.O.)

          (on the T.V.)

        Protesters on both sides of the Gay Rights issue have

        been outside the White House all day today:

She goes to the window and sees her other dog, Mr. Sasha Fu (a German Shepard/Pit) outside in
the backyard sunbathing.

                                                        CUT TO:

TELEVISION: TV NEWS CAST

Conservative # 1 is holding a SIGN which reads: MARRIAGE IS BETWEEN A MAN AND A

WOMAN!

CONSERVATIVE PROTESTER # 1

(on the T.V.)

Marriage is between a man and a woman. Homosexuality
is a sin and anyone who   participates in homosexual
activities is going to burn in Hell!

LIBERAL PROTESTER # 1

(on the T.V.)

This is America! We all must have the right to be
free to do what we like with our own bodies as well
as other consenting bodies.

A conservative is arguing with a liberal...

CONSERVATIVE PROTESTER # 2

(on the T.V.)

All gay's should be killed! It's immoral in the eyes
of God.

LIBERAL PROTESTER # 2

(angrily)

That's for God to decide. Have more faith in your
God and mind your own damn business!

A protester off to the side of the crowd of fellow protesters...

LIBERAL PROTESTER # **3**

(on the T.V.)

The religious right must remember that God is the

only judge and the Conservatives must remember,

separation of church and state. The bottom line is that

the only thing Gay Marriage hurts, are the ego's of

immature and irrational people.

AEHLEX (laughs)

(talking to herself, the TV and Honey)

Yeah, NO SHIT! I can't believe how ridiculous people

are. My God. It's just so stupid, it's maddening. I must

be in the twilight zone. Nothing on this planet makes any

damn sense.

(looks up)

Ahh.. beam me up. Please! I wanna' come home. ...

SFX: THE PHONE RINGS.

Aehlex grabs the Television remote, mutes the T.V. and answers the phone.

AEHLEX

Speak! (pause) Hey, what's up? (pause) No, I just
got up. (pause) Ok, Cool. Sounds like a plan. I'll
see you soon.

She hangs up and looks at Honey.

AEHLEX

You wanna go for a ride in the car?

Honey wiggles her body and tail in excitement.

EXT ~ STREETS OF LOS ANGELES ~ DRIVING ~ DAY

MUSIC: The very beginning of Smashing Pumpkins' song 'Silver Fuck' has begun playing.

Aehlex is now dressed and driving from Venice to Larchmont Ave in Hancock Park. She is
driving a brown 1988 Oldsmobile Cutlass Ciera with tented windows while listening to the
Smashing Pumpkins song 'Silver Fuck' on her car radio. Honey is also in the car.

NARRATION : AEHLEX'S VOICE OVER (MUSIC IS STILL PLAYING IN BG): " *My
name is Alexis Nichele Pauling but my close friends call me Aehlex. I was born in Santa Monica,
CA and raised in Hollywood. I guess I can say I have been bored with this life for as long as I
can remember. Ironically, I have had more interesting things happen in my life than in most
movies.*"

FLASH BACK TO AUGUST 14TH, 1975

INT ~ SAINT JOHN'S MEDICAL CENTER ~ SANTA MONICA, CA.

A NEWBORN, AEHLEX lies in a see thru crib in the maternity ward nursery with all the other newborns.

AEHLEX'S VO: *"I've been freaking people out ever since I arrived on this planet. My mother told me that the day after I was born, I was already lifting my head up and looking around like a turtle ".*

Show newborn Aehlex lifting her head to look around.

A nurse comes in and sees Aehlex looking around, she almost drops a tray she is carrying. The FEMALE NURSE IS AFRICAN-AMERICAN, heavy set and middle-aged.

Music volume lowers.

FEMALE NURSE

Craig! Come here. Hurry up.

Craig, a male nurse, quickly swings around the corner.

MALE NURSE

What?

The female nurse point's to baby Aehlex in her crib.

MALE NURSE

Holy crap!

FEMALE NURSE

(shaking her head)

I've been doin this a long time and I've never seen

a newborn do that before.

FLASH BACK ENDS

EXTERIOR - LARCHMONT AVE, L.A. CA - DAY

Aehlex and Honey pull into a metered parking spot directly in front of their destination, a
restaurant.

They exit the vehicle, pay the meter and walk over to an occupied outside table where Trent sits
waiting.

Trent is about 5'6", thin, Blonde, cute and wears glasses. He is one of Aehlex's closest friends.

AEHLEX

Hey you.

Aehlex and Trent Kiss on the cheek.

TRENT

Hey.

    (looks down and speaks in a baby voice)

Hi Honey.

    (looks back at Aehlex)

I see you got Rock Star parking as usual.

AEHLEX

As usual. Thank You parking fairies. I've got the
best parking fairies ever. I'm telling you, you need
to get some parking fairies.

TRENT

    (laughing)

Parking fairies.

AEHLEX

Go ahead and laugh but I rarely ever have parking
issues.

TRENT

That's true. Hmmm…

AEHLEX

Uh huh, that's alright. No one ever listens to me until
it's too late.

WAITER

Are you ready to order?

TRENT

I'm ready. Do you know what you want?

AEHLEX

Yes, I want Salmon, Tuna, Unagi And California
Rolls to start please.

TRENT

And I want Sashimi Salmon, California rolls and
Miso soup please.

WAITER

Would you like anything to drink?

AEHLEX

Uhhh ..can you please bring us a large hot Sake and

water?

(looks down at Honey)

Oh and would it be possible to bring her

water too please?

The waiter grabs Trent's menu.

WAITER

Sure.

Aehlex hands the waiter her menu and smiles.

AEHLEX

Thank You very much.

TRENT

(lights a cigarette)

Thank You.

The waiter walks away.

TRENT

What are you doing tomorrow?

AEHLEX

Extra work. I'm working regularly now on that new

T.V. show I told you about.

TRENT

The one about A&R guys starring that raunchy comedian?

AEHLEX

Yep. "The Biz" I've got to be there at the crack of

dawn. It's cool though because I get to meet different

famous musicians every Tuesday. But I think I'm

gonna have to stop doing extra work soon before I

have to kill someone for being disrespectful to me.

It's just so damn degrading! Not only do they pay us

shit, but when they're not treating us like we're bad

children, they treat us like dirt. Ironically, their movies

and shows would look really lame without us. But I

can understand how extra's get a bad rap. Some of

them are really crazy.

Trent laughs.

                    AEHLEX

No, seriously. No one does background checks on

background actors. As a matter of fact it is common

knowledge that people who get out of prison and

mental institutions are told to go work as extras.

                    TRENT

Are you serious? That doesn't sound like the safest

environment. You would think they'd make it harder

since you're working so closely with celebrities.

                    AEHLEX

Yeah, you would think but that would cost too much

money. Who's gonna pay for it? And the 'on set'

security is a joke. I remember being on set one day

with this woman who just didn't seem right to us.

The woman kept giving this really sweet girl named Iris,

attitude. So of course the girl comes crying to me even

though I didn't know her.

TRENT

Of course.

AEHLEX

Of course. So, being the person I am, I proceeded to
give the woman dirty looks just to let her know that I
was watching her. She finally left Iris alone. Later that
week both Iris and I saw the woman on Hard Copy.

TRENT

What???

Aehlex and Trent both get distracted as two super hot guys walk buy.

AEHLEX

Yeah, umm... umm oh ya, well apparently the woman
had just gotten out of prison after three years for stalking
Michael J. Fox.

TRENT

And then she's back on set.. that's not good.

AEHLEX

Yeah, exactly. So Iris called Simply Casting and asked
if they were aware that they were booking Michael J.
Fox's stalker. But because she didn't know the woman's
name, they just said there was nothing they could do.

TRENT

That's ridiculous! Basically what they're saying is that
they're going to wait until someone dies before they do
anything. That's typical, well be careful tomorrow.
Do you know which musicians will be there?

AEHLEX

No. I never know until I get to set. Last week I met
Eric Sermon. Do you remember him, the green eyed
bandit.?

TRENT

Yes. He sang that song 'Stay real'. I actually saw him
in concert once.

AEHLEX

That's cool. I don't really like crowds unless I'm on
stage, so I don't really go to concerts much. Although,
I'd love to go see Jane's Addiction but the tickets have
been sold out for weeks.

TRENT

I'd love to go to a Fishbone concert. I really want to
meet those guys.

AEHLEX

I don't know anything about Fishbone but I have
heard of them.

TRENT

I love Fishbone! They Rock! When are you working
at the bookstore again?

AEHLEX

Friday, Saturday and Sunday. I got the weekend shift
this month. I've gotta quit that job too. That place
attracts way too much craziness.

TRENT

Girrrl.. You can't quit both your jobs! How are you
gonna eat?

AEHLEX

I don't know, I'll figure it out but it's time to move on,
ya know. I mean luckily I am the person I am and I can
handle the madness and the disrespect but why should I
if I'm not happy? For money? I don't think so.

The waiter brings their food & drinks.

AEHLEX

Although it is nice to eat.

WAITER

I'll be right back with her water.

The waiter walks away.

AEHLEX

Oh yeah, thank you! Yay food! Yeah it is nice to eat.

It's also nice to have a roof over my head. I never want

to be homeless again.

TRENT

(pouring sake)

No we definitely don't want that. Cheers.

Trent raises his glass.

Aehlex raises her glass.

AEHLEX

L'chiam.

They both drink.

AEHLEX

So, I was just watching the news and I can not believe

that there is such a big debate going on over gay marriage.

It's so ridiculous! It's not even a social issue. It's a

religious issue.

TRENT

I know. What ever happened to the separation between

church and state?

AEHLEX

Exactly. That was established to protect those who

practice religion as well as those who do not, in this

so called free country. If the Christians and Catholics

want to say, no you can't get married in our church,

that's one thing. But they have absolutely no right to

dictate whether or not gays can be married by a judge.

Besides even convicts are allowed to marry.

TRENT

(eating)

I know it sends a great message. Doesn't it?

AEHLEX

(eating)

That's basically saying that homosexuals are worse

than criminals simply because they are homosexual.

That's terrible!

TRENT

Convicts can marry and convicted murders can adopt

children but gays can't marry or adopt children, in

Florida.

AEHLEX

That's ridiculous! It's madness! (sighs) Whatever,

heterosexuals are just worried that gays will be better

at marriage and make them look bad.

TRENT

(laughs)

You're probably right.

The waiter brings Honey's water.

AEHLEX

(to the waiter)

Thank You.

TRENT

Oh yeah, not to change the subject or anything but...

AEHLEX

(still upset over gay topic)

Please, go ahead ..I'm done.

A WOMAN walks by with a BEAGLE on a leash. Honey begins to whine. Aehlex looks down at
Honey and over to the woman walking the beagle.

AEHLEX

(to Honey)

That looks like your boyfriend Sunny B. Doesn't it ,girlie?

(to Trent)

Beagles are her favorite. Anyway, you were saying...

TRENT

(excited)

I was just gonna say, (pause) I got our Amsterdam

tickets this morning!!

AEHLEX

(excited)

Nice! I can't wait! Six more months. Amsterdam is

my favorite place in the world. You are gonna love it!

I always feel as if I have entered a different dimension

when I'm in Amsterdam. There's so much magic there.

And the Dutch are so efficient. One of my Dutch friends

once told me that since everything is built on canals,

every few years or so the buildings begin to sink so they

actually take the entire building apart piece by piece

and rebuild it. They even use the same materials.

Unless a roof shingle is cracked or something, then they

replace it. Isn't that crazy?

TRENT

Interesting. You wouldn't expect such things from a

place where drugs are legal.

AEHLEX

I know. The world could learn a lot from the Dutch.

Oh my God, I can't wait! I can't wait!

(looks at Honey)

Although, I am really gonna miss my girl. And as

much as I love to travel, I always get homesick pretty

quick. There's no place like home.

INT ~ SET OF 'THE BIZ' ~ SOUNDSTAGE ~ AUDIENCE BLEACHERS ~ MORNING

Adam & Aehlex walk back on the sound stage over to the extra's holding area, climb the steps to the audience bleachers (holding) and sits near two other extra's, Carrie and Steven, whom Aehlex and Adam do not know. There are about 20 extra's in the holding area.

Carrie is a very beautiful young Caucasian female, 20, who is Vegan and into raves & Burning Man.

Steven is about 30, sandy blonde hair, light eyes, very thin, a bit nerdy, wears glasses.

All the extra's are dressed like hip trendsetters.

ADAM

Is anyone sitting here?

CARRIE

I don't think so.

AEHLEX

(friendly)

Cool. Hi, I'm Alexis and this is Adam.

127

CARRIE

(to Aehlex)

Nice to meet you. I love your name. Is it short for

Alexandra?

AEHLEX

No. That's a misconception. Alexis is a totally separate

Name however Alexandra and Alexis both mean defender

of mankind. My good friends call me Aehlex for short.

CARRIE

(smiles)

Aehlex. That's cool, how do you spell it?

AEHLEX

A .e. h. l .e .x. I had to invent the spelling.

CARRIE

Nice.. by the way, I'm Carrie.

STEVEN

(smiles)

And I'm Steven.

AEHLEX

It's nice to meet you both. Have you two been doing

extra work long?

CARRIE

This is my first day.

AEHLEX

Really? Nice! Well stick with us kid and you'll be

alright.

ADAM

Yeah, we'll show you the ropes. It's easy.

STEVEN

I've been doin this for about a year now. I also perform

as a clown at children's parties.

ADAM

(laughs)

That's cool.

                    AEHLEX

    (to Adam)

Duuuude! How much do I love you right now? Oh

my God! You have no idea. I'm sooo excited!

    (to Carrie and Steven)

Adam just told me that he has an extra Jane's Addiction

ticket for Thursday night.

                    CARRIE

That's awesome! Those tickets have been sold out

for weeks.

                    AEHLEX

I know I can hardly believe it.

                    CARRIE

I should probably go to the restroom now since rehearsal's

gonna start any minute, right?

                    AEHLEX

Yeah, go now just incase, but they never start on time

here. Get used to this fraise, "hurry up and wait" because

you'll be hearing and feeling that a lot doing extra work.

Carrie stands up to leave.

CARRIE

I'll be right back.

Carrie walks away.

STEVEN

So you guys have worked on this show before?

ADAM

Aehlex and I are regulars. We are here every week.

AEHLEX

(looks over at a girl walking toward her)

Cool, here comes Lisa. I was just wondering where

she was.

Lisa is also very cute, young, Caucasian, 19. She is dressed like a Go Go dancer.

LISA

(happily)

What's up?

AEHLEX

Girrrl, I was startin to think you weren't comin'.

Lisa puts her bag on one of the chairs.

LISA

I was in wardrobe forever. They couldn't decide if

they wanted me to be a waitress or a Go Go dancer.

Are you goin' with me tonight?

AEHLEX

Yep it will be fun. I had a good time last week.

ADAM

Where are you guys goin' tonight?

AEHLEX

The producers and cast of a couple of different shows,

go to Vino every Tuesday night. And since my girl

Lisa here is friends with one of the producers, she gets

AEHLEX (CONT'D)

to go too. I'm just fortunate enough to be allowed

to tag along.

ADAM

That's cool.

AEHLEX

Yeah, I ran into Andy Dick again last week. That kid is crazy.

I totally thought that I was gonna get myself fired

hangin out with him. Not that we were doing anything

wrong, we were just having too much fun while

everyone else was being all uppity and conservative.

LISA

Yeah, well I'm sure that walk you guys took outside

helped loosen you up.

AEHLEX

(smiling devilishly)

Yes, walking is good. Very, very good. Ah shit! I totally

forgot that I signed up for open mic poetry, tonight at

Swivel. Damn! I can't flake. I'm meeting people there.

LISA

That's cool, you can go to Vino with me again next week.

Or, every week, really.

AEHLEX

That's true.

LISA

Did I miss any of your crazy stories?

AEHLEX

Nooo.

STEVEN

What crazy stories?

ADAM

(smugly)

Alexis tells crazy stories. She says their true but I

don't know.

STEVEN

Like what?

(like a child)

Will you please tell me bedtime a story?

AEHLEX

Sure, but it might give you nightmares.

Carrie returns and sits down.

STEVEN

You got back just in time.

CARRIE

Why? What's going on?

LISA

Aehlex is gonna tell one of her freaky stories.

AEHLEX

Alright I'll tell one I haven't told b4. O.K, so I have

come to understand that it is really easy for demonic

energies to temporarily take over the bodies of instable

human beings. For example, If a person's on serious

drugs or Schizophrenic or something, it is very easy to

manipulate their electromagnetic energy if you have the

right tools and knowledge. I know this all sounds crazy

but I never believed in demons or Satan until the ugly

& dark energies introduced themselves to me. Most

of these entities I have not feared and that in itself forces

them to keep some distance. However, there was one in

particular who did frighten me. I was living with one of

The Mystic Eye psychics at the time. The Mystic Eye is

the new age bookstore that I work at in Venice. It was

just after ten O'clock at night and I was driving up to the

apartment when suddenly I saw a man standing on the corner.

FLASHBACK

EXTERIOR ~ PENMAR AVE ~ VENICE STREET ~ FALL (NOV) 1998 ~ NIGHT

Aehlex pulls up to the corner where the man is standing, turns left then makes a u-turn and parks only 15 feet away from the strange person.

The man is tall and brown and has very unusual glowing kryptonite green eyes. It was as if I were suddenly in a movie.

NARRATION: AEHLEX'S VOICE OVER *"As I made a left at the corner our eyes met. He never took his eyes off of me. The strangest thing about the man was that he had glowing kryptonite green eyes. Right away I knew that he was a demon. As I began to park I heard a male voice in my head. One of my guardians."*

MALE VOICE

He's waiting for you.

AEHLEX

(aggravated)

I don't care who he's waiting for! I don't know him.

I'm exhausted and I'm going home.

Just before Aehlex turns her car off the strange man begins to quickly walk toward her. Suddenly Aehlex becomes terrified.

AEHLEX

He really is waiting for me. Shit!

She puts her car in reverse and drives off.

FLASHBACK ENDS.

AEHLEX

I know that the man was going to kill me. I have
never been so scared.

ADAM

You said he had glowing green eyes. What the fuck
is that all about?

AEHLEX

All I know was as soon as I saw those eyes I knew
that he was a demon. I'm always surprised at how
calmly I usually react to all of this stuff. But I'm
an ancient soul so I've seen it all before. I just don't
have much conscious memory of these things until I
am reminded with a new experience in this life and
body.

STEVEN

So you hear voices?

AEHLEX

I always hear my guardians very loudly and clearly whenever my life is in danger. Once while driving home I had said to my car... "I know something's wrong with you, although I can't put my finger on it and you're not showing any signs of a problem, I can FEEL it". So, I get home, it's 3am & two music producers I didn't know were sitting on my couch waiting for me.

ADAM

(laughs)

Did you often find random guys on your couch at 3am?

AEHLEX

Yeah, actually I would. My ex-roommate owns a recording studio. She had invited the two producers over to meet me.

STEVEN

(to Aehlex)

Are you a singer?

AEHLEX

Sometimes. Anyway, as these two producers rambled on about music I heard a voice say, "the problem with your car is that your fuel injectors are leaking. You can no longer drive your car".

CARRIE

What? Seriously?

AEHLEX

I'm totally serious. I'm not makin any of this stuff up. I remember being sober and thinking I was delirious so I told the producers that I was delirious and had to go to bed. The next day I went out to move my car for street cleaning. I remembered what I had heard the night b4 and popped the hood. Ironically my mechanic had just showed me where my fuel injectors were days before. Sure enough there was gasoline all over my engine. I sat on the ground and cried for fifteen minutes. It made me nervous but It all worked out of course.

(she looks up)

Thanx again guys!!!

LISA

That's crazy!

STEVEN

I'm going to have nightmares about the guy with the
glowing green eyes.

ADAM

(laughing)

Me too. That's what I was just thinking.

AEHLEX

Yeah, well how do you think I felt. I'd only heard
voices telepathically a few times at that point. But
I'll tell you what, when these things do occur I'm
finally excited and not totally bored with life like
I usually am. But seriously, if I can experience all

AEHLEX (CONT'D)

these crazy things and still walk around alone without
fear, then I think you'll be ok.

The 2nd A.D. walks over to the extra's holding area.

2nd A.D.

We need everyone on set for rehearsal.

All the extra's stand up sporadically and begin to walk over to the set.

EXTERIOR - THE MYSTIC EYE BOOKSTORE - MORNING

TITLE ~ 6 months later

MUSIC: Stone Temple Pilots song 'Meat plow' is playing.

Aehlex pulls into a parking spot on the side of the building. On the front of the store is a huge sign that says The Mystic Eye Bookstore. She gets out of the car, walks over to the front door and unlocks it. Aehlex can see a new employee, Jonahs, walking down the street.

Jonahs is a cute, young, dark haired man with blue eyes, jewelry and piercings. He is 20 and an artist. He often wears very colorful pants but he is mostly Goth at heart. He walks into the bookstore right after Aehlex.

Aehlex is behind the counter at the stereo, putting in Jane's Addictions Ritual CD.

AEHLEX

(jovial)

Good morning.

JONAHS

(sleepy)

Good morning.

AEHLEX

Hey, do you drink coffee?

JONAHS

Yes, I do. Actually, I was just thinkin' bout coffee.

AEHLEX

Well, that doesn't surprise me. I must have heard ya.

I think I'm gonna go down the street and get some

coffee as soon as Jeanette gets here. One of us

usually does a coffee run in the morning. So are you

ready for your 'Eye' adventure?

JONAHS

I think so.. but from what I hear, I'm not so sure.

AEHLEX

This is definitely a very unique environment.

Between the spirits, demons, psychics and celebrities,

It's pretty crazy. But it is a lot of fun.

JONAHS

Celebrities?

AEHLEX

Yeah, we get a few from time to time. Ok I'll tell you
a quick story. Three weeks before I began working
here I got lucky and came across a Jane's Addiction
ticket.

JONAHS

For that relapse tour?

AEHLEX

Yep, for that sold out relapse tour. At the time I
only knew three of their songs but I was already
addicted. I was told that Perry Farrell would come
in here from time to time, so I would play Jane's
Addiction really loudly every morning hoping that
Perry would pick up on it psychically and come in
to the store. Three weeks after I first started working
here, Perry came in. He invited me to his studio
and then we became friends. He spins at Saint Martin's
sometimes on Sunday. I'll let you know when, if
you're interested.

JONAHS

Are you serious?

AEHLEX

Dead. I know it's crazy, huh? What's even crazier is
that Jeanette's favorite band came in the very next day.

JONAHS

Who's Jeanette's favorite band?

AEHLEX

Aerosmith.

JONAHS

That's crazy.

AEHLEX

Yeah, that was only the beginning. A lot of strange
things have happened to me since I started working
here. My first day at The Eye was quite interesting.
I discovered very quickly that I was in for an adventure.

FLASHBACK

INTERIOR ~ THE MYSTIC EYE MANAGER'S OFFICE ~RAINY AFTERNOON

Jeanette is the manager. She is sitting behind her desk holding Aehlex's application. Jeanette is short, with dark hair, blue eyes, and super cute. She is about 30 years old.

Aehlex is sitting on the other side of the desk.

JEANETTE

So, can you start tomorrow?

AEHLEX

Ahh, sure. What time?

JEANETTE

Well, it would be good for you to open so be here at 9:30. We open at 10:00a.m.

AEHLEX

Ok. I look forward to it. It will also be nice to see the sun again tomorrow.

JEANETTE

They said on the news that it won't stop raining until Wednesday.

                              AEHLEX

     (smiles)

Yeah well, Gaea told me Tuesday. So we should

see some sun tomorrow.

                             JEANETTE

That would be nice after 10 days of rain.

                              AEHLEX

     (playfully)

Don't you mean that will be nice? Have you forgotten

who you are dealing with, woman? You've known me

way to long to be doubtful.

                             JEANETTE

     (playfully)

Oh yeah, that's right. Sorry.

                              AEHLEX

     (playfully)

It's ok. Just don't let it happen again.

                             JEANETTE

     (playfully)

Ok. I won't.

AEHLEX

(smiling)

Good. Ok, I'll see you in the morning. Thank You.

Aehlex leaves the store.

INTERIOR ~ THE MYSTIC EYE BOOKSTORE ~ VENICE,CA ~ MORNING

The sun is shining.

Aehlex enters the store. The counter is to the right of the entrance.

Behind the counter is Jessica, a portly black girl about 25 years old wearing black and a **pentagram** around her neck. Jess wears **gothic jewelry**. She is counting the money in the cash register.

MUSIC: Audio Slave's song 'Set it Off' is playing loudly.

AEHLEX

Good morning.

JESSICA

(turns the music down)

You must be Alexis.

147

                              AEHLEX

          Yep and you must be Jessica.

                              JESSICA

          That's me. Jeanette is in her office.

                              AEHLEX

          Ok, cool. Thanx. I'll be back in a minute. Cool

          music by the way.

Jessica just smiles & turns the music back up.

INT ~ THE MYSTIC EYE BOOKSTORE ~ THE ATTIC ~ VENICE, CA ~ MORNING

Aehlex walks toward the back of the store to Jeanette's office and knocks on the partially open

door.

                              AEHLEX

          Good morning.

                              JEANETTE

              (smiling)

          Good morning. You were right. The sun's out.

                              AEHLEX

          Thank Gaea!

JEANETTE

Did you meet Jessica yet?

AEHLEX

Yes. I just did.

JEANETTE

Shane's here too but he went to get coffee. So if you

don't mind I'd like you to vacuum the main room.

AEHLEX

Ok. No problem.

JEANETTE

Just ask Jess to show you where the vacuum is.

AEHLEX

OBKB.

Aehlex walks to the front counter where she finds Jess and Shane.

Shane is also portly. He is Caucasian, has **a goatee** and **a pony tale**. He also wears a lot of black

has some **piercings** and a **pentagram** around his neck. He is holding a cup of coffee. He is 25.

AEHLEX

Hello.

                              JESSICA

        Shane this is Alexis. Alexis, Shane.

                              SHANE

              (to Aehlex)

        Welcome to our nightmare.

                              AEHLEX

        Thanx.

                              JESSICA

              (hits Shane)

        Shut up!

                              JESSICA

              (to Aehlex)

        Don't listen to him. This job is fun.

                              SHANE

        Yeah. Fun for a witch.

Aehlex just gives him a subtle yet suspicious look.

                              AEHLEX

        Jessica can you please show me where you guys keep

        the vacuum cleaner?

JESSICA

Sure it's in the Attic closet.

The Attic is the used part of the bookstore where used books and items are sold. Directly connected to the main bookstore it is the mellow side of the bookstore. Both the main side and attic have different stereo systems. The lights are out and the stereo is off.

Jess comes around the corner opens the closet door and flips the closet lights on.

JESSICA

Here's the vacuum. The aprons are in here too but

you don't have to put one on until we open.

Jess hands Aehlex the vacuum and walks over to the counter where the stereo and cash register are.

AEHLEX

Thanx.

Aehlex grabs the vacuum and closes the closet door.

JESSICA

I've gotta turn on the Attic stereo and count the

drawer but Shane will show you where all the plugs

are on the main side.

INT ~ THE MYSTIC EYE BOOKSTORE ~ MAIN SIDE ~ VENICE, CA ~ MORNING

Shane is straitening books nearby and over hears Jess. When Alexis comes around the corner he simply point's to a large armored knight statue against the wall.

                              SHANE
            (smiles)
            The best plugs are behind the big statues.

                              AEHLEX
            (smiles)
            Gracias.

Aehlex walks over, plugs the vacuum in behind the armored night statue and begins to vacuum.

Shane walks over to the stereo and skips back to song # 2 'Show me how to live' and cranks it up.

MUSIC: Audio Slave 'Show me how to live'

Aehlex just smiles and sings along as she vacuum's and discovers the many odd & different items for sale at The Mystic Eye. Voodoo dolls, gems, oils, incense, statues, herbs, books, oujia boards, massage tools, tarot cards, tarot bags, deities, candles etc...

SFX: THEN THE PHONE RINGS.

Shane turns down the music.

Aehlex hears the phone, looks up and turns off the vacuum.

Jess fly's around the corner.

JESSICA

Don't answer that! We're not open yet!

SHANE

I know but it might be my wife.

(Answers the phone)

Good morning the Mystic Eye. (Pause).... I won't

be sure which psychics will be here until 10am

when we open. Can you call back then?.. (pause)....

Well so far I know that Sunrise will be here and so will

Athena but I won't know who else will be here until 10

if you'd like to call back then.

Jess walks over to the main counter where Shane is on the phone.

JESSICA

(smiling & poking at Shane)

I told you not to answer the phone.

Jess sticks her tongue at Shane.

Shane just smiles.

SHANE
(patiently but annoyed)

Sunrise is very clairvoyant where as Athena is

more clairaudient and telepathic but they both use

tarot cards. Call back in a half hour and schedule

an appointment ok.

Shane hangs up the phone.

SHANE

These psychic junkies are so crazy! Jesus!

Aehlex smiles and continues to vacuum. She vacuums past about 50 image candles (image candles of penis' and vagina's, men and woman etc) on the middle shelf of a 1½ ft deep bookcase against a wall to her right. She vacuums down the middle of the aisle as the cord is on the floor all the way to the left. As soon as her back is to the image candles she hears a loud crashing sound. She quickly turns around and finds all the image candles (aprox. 40-50 candles) lying face down on the floor all spread out.

AEHLEX

What the hell?

Aehlex hears Jess giggle from behind the cash counter but pays little attention.

She then carefully and patiently re-stacks the candles back onto the shelf. When finished, she goes back to vacuuming. As soon as her back is to the candles and she turns the vacuum on, she hears a loud crash. She turns around and finds all of the image candles back on the floor. She turns the vacuum cleaner off.

AEHLEX

(perplexed)

What the fuck?!

Jess and Shane are standing behind the main counter about 15 feet away, giggling.

What the fuck is going on & what's so funny?

Aehlex bends down to re-stack the candles once more. Jessica and Shane walk over to her.

JESSICA

Oh that's George.

AEHLEX

Who the fuck is George?

JESSICA

George is one of the spirits who lives here. He gets
upset if you don't say hi to him when you come in.

SHANE

It's part of George's new comer initiation.

AEHLEX

Oh. Ok. Well thanx for telling me. Hello George.

Nice to meet you. I'm Alexis.

(to Jessica)

So what's George's story?

JESSICA

George is cool. He helps us get rid of bad spirits.

SHANE

Some of the psychics believe that he owned this land

back when it was farmland. He died of a heart attack

and never left.

AEHLEX

Interesting. And who named him George?

SHANE

(sarcastically)

His momma.

Jess walks over to the armored knight.

JESSICA

(laughs)

He told a few of our psychics that his name is George.
We also named this guy George because this is where
we believe he hides.

AEHLEX

Right on. That's cool. But I do recall you saying that
George was only one of the spirits that lives here. Who
else do I need to introduce myself to?

JESSICA

Well there's also Mary who doesn't come around
too much but sometimes people do see her briefly,
wearing a long white flowing dress.. Bobby is the
kid and the thief.

SHANE

But George is the boss. He's the most present. Mary
is the least present and Bobby only comes around
every now and again.

AEHLEX

What do you mean the kid's a thief?

SHANE

He's more like a magician. He makes things disappear

and then re-appear in strange places or strange ways.

AEHLEX

(happily)

Crazy. Ohhh this jobs gonna be fun!

JESSICA

(looks at Shane)

I like her, she ain't right.

SHANE

Yeah, you're alright.

Jeanette comes around the corner holding a large scheduling book. She walks over to the main

counter and puts the book down.

Aehlex is still re-stacking the candles.

JEANETTE

(to Shane & Jessica)

Can you guys put the signs out?

SHANE

Yes mam.

JESSICA

(to Jeanette)

Alexis just met George.

Aehlex, still kneeling down while re-stacking, stands up.

AEHLEX

(to Jeanette)

Yeah, thanx for the warning.

(laughs)

I've been coming in here for years and you've never

said anything to me about George.

JEANETTE

(giggles)

What happened?

AEHLEX

Twice, while I was vacuuming, all those candles of

people and private parts kept shooting out off the shelf.

JEANETTE

Oh the image candles. Weird!

159

AEHLEX

Yeah. Really Weird. The first time it happened, I

thought that maybe the vacuum cord did it but the

image candles are up on the middle shelf & the cord

is near all the long skinny candles, come look.

Aehlex is still standing by the candles.

Jeanette walks over to her. She points out the depth of the shelf.

Every time I would walk by with the vacuum, all

of these candles would end up spread out on the

floor face down. See where the cord is.

JEANETTE

Yep. Weird.

AEHLEX

And Jess and Shane were too far away to have time

to run over, knock all the candles out and run back

before I could catch them

JEANETTE

Well that's George.

FLASH BACK ENDS

Aehlex is still standing near the stereo about to play the Jane's Addiction CD.

> **JONAHS**
>
> (smiling)
>
> George, huh?
>
> (looks around)
>
> I'm Jonahs. It's very nice to meet you.

> **AEHLEX**
>
> I think George likes you so you're gonna be alright.
>
> I hope you like Jane's.

Jonahs shakes his head yes and gives Aehlex an approving look.

Aehlex plays Jane's Addiction. 'Whores' comes on loudly. She grabs glass cleaner and paper towels from behind the counter and hands it to Jonahs.

MUSIC: 'Whores' Jane's Addiction Kettle Whistle CD

> **AEHLEX**
>
> (Yells)
>
> Can you clean all the glass cases, please?

Jonahs responds with a nod of his head and a smile.

INT ~ THE MYSTIC EYE BOOKSTORE ~ ATTIC ~ VENICE, CA ~ MORNING

Aehlex walks into the Attic and grabs the vacuum out of the closet.

MUSIC: There is no music on in the Attic so 'Whore's can still be heard well although a little muted.

While in the Attic she also gets two cash envelopes out of the safe. She takes one envelope to the Attic cash register, passing by the wall of Saints and the table with three (normal) candles. She then takes the vacuum and other cash envelope to the main side of the store.

INT ~ THE MYSTIC EYE BOOKSTORE ~ MAIN SIDE ~ SAME MORNING

MUSIC: 'Whores' is still playing on the stereo

Aehlex leaves the vacuum near the counter. She walks back behind the counter & begins counting the cash into the cash register while dancing & singing along with the music.

About 10 seconds later, Jeanette walks in hyper and giggling and quickly closes and locks the door behind her.

Aehlex turns the music down.

AEHLEX

Oh no, what is it? Or I should say, who is it?

Jeanette goes behind the counter and sits down in a chair across from where Aehlex is standing.

JEANETTE

(giggling)

The warlock.

AEHLEX

Oh no. It's too early for the warlock. We'll let Jonahs

handle him.

Jonahs walks over to the counter holding the glass cleaner and paper towels.

JONAHS

Who's the warlock?

AEHLEX

Someone we hide from.

JEANETTE

This crazy old homeless guy who loves Alexis.

AEHLEX

Yeah. When we first met he would always jump at me

and try to scare me but it never worked so then he

163

fell in love with me. I don't know. He's funny.

He walks around telling everybody he's a warlock

JEANETTE

Yesterday, we saw him coming and we both dove

under the counter all huddled together.

AEHLEX

Yeah ,we were rockin back and forth tryin not to laugh

hysterically because he was standing there talkin to

himself. Talkin' bout,

    (spoken very darkly)

"I am, the warlock".

JEANETTE

    (laughing)

That was so funny.

AEHLEX

It was pretty funny. Shit! I wanna go get coffee.

Where did you see him?

JEANETTE

Walking towards Rose.

AEHLEX

Cool, then maybe I can get some coffee before I run

into any crazies today.

JEANETTE

Yeah right. Good luck.

AEHLEX

Thanx. You want the usual?

JEANETTE

Yes please.

AEHLEX

(yells)

Jonahs, how do you like your coffee? Do you want

me to bring you back some cream and sugar?

JONAHS

Yes, please. Here's some money.

AEHLEX

No worries. We got it.

JEANETTE

Since it's your first day, we'll treat.

                              AEHLEX

              Alright, I'll be back in a minute.

Aehlex walks out the front door and down Main St.

EXTERIOR - MAIN ST. VENICE/ SANTA MONICA, CA - MORNING

The sun is shining. Aehlex is walking North on the East side of Main St. to the Coffee House. She

runs into her homeless friend Bryan ,who begins to walk with her.

Bryan is a homeless African-American vet, 40ish and in a wheelchair. He is wearing headphones

and a camouflage army jacket.

                              BRYAN

              Hey you.

                              AEHLEX

              Good morning. Sir, how are you?

                              BRYAN

              I'm lovin my new walkman. Thank you guys so much.

                              AEHLEX

              No worries. I was upset that someone had stolen your

radio. So I told everyone at work ,and I said, "ya know, there's a lot of things I could live without but music isn't one of them." They agreed and we all pitched in. Now we just got to get you out of that wheelchair and into an apartment.

                    BRYAN

The doctors say that I have a 50/50 Chance of walking again.

                    AEHLEX

Yeah well, I think that you have a 70% chance. God told me 70%.

                    BRYAN

I'd have to go to Texas to get the surgery but I don't know about all that.

                    AEHLEX

Well, I see you walkin' again. I don't know when. But I definitely do see you walking again.

Aehlex suddenly spots the warlock coming straight toward her.

                    AEHLEX

        (grins)

Oh no, it's the warlock. Just be cool. He's crazy.

167

The warlock is a Caucasian man in his 50's with grayish/white hair and beard. His hair is in a pony tale. He looks like a small old biker.

THE WARLOCK

(to Bryan)

Hey, hey you be good to her! She's cool.

Bryan just stares at him.

AEHLEX

(to the warlock)

He's cool. It's all good. This is my good friend Bryan.

Bryan, the warlock.

The warlock bends down and gets in Bryan's face.

THE WARLOCK

I am, The Warlock. Look into my eyes!

Bryan gives The Warlock a dirty look.

AEHLEX

(laughs)

Ok.... We gotta go now. It was nice

see'n ya man.

Aehlex and Bryan walk/roll away.

The Warlock walks in the opposite direction.

AEHLEX

I told you. He's crazy. The other day he was telling

me something about eating the heart of a ten year

old boy or something.

BRYAN

Shit. He just better leave me alone.

INT ~ STRIDER'S HOUSE ~ VENICE, CA ~ NIGHT

Aehlex walks into Strider's house. The door is unlocked.

Strider is in his loft which is in his bedroom. He sleeps on a mattress on the floor of the loft. The

loft is small and has an awkward low ceiling. There is also an entire galaxy of glow in the dark

stars painted on all the walls and ceiling. All the lights are off except for the glow in the dark

stars. There is a ladder screwed into the wall leading up to the square hole in the ceiling.

INT ~ STRIDER'S BEDROOM ~ VENICE, CA ~ NIGHT

Aehlex enters Strider's bedroom.

AEHLEX

Hey.

Aehlex climbs the loft ladder.

INT ~ STRIDER'S LOFT ~ VENICE, CA ~ NIGHT

Strider is writing with a reading light clamped to his book. He is sitting in the corner on his bed which is on the floor.

Aehlex looks around at the stars. She climbs most of the way in and sits on the floor with her legs hanging out of the hatch.

AEHLEX

Wow, this is so cool. Did you do this?

STRIDER

(writing in a journal)

I decided to create my own galaxy.

AEHLEX

Nice.

STRIDER

(gruffly)

So what's up?

Strider turns the reading light off, closes his journal & looks up.

AEHLEX

I just had another telepathic experience last night. But this one I just don't understand at all. I mean I'm not sure where it came from or why.

STRIDER

What was it?

AEHLEX

Well, I had just lay down on my bed and closed my eyes when suddenly I hear Perry's voice say, "Alexis, go to Saint Martin's tonight, I'll be there alone at midnight." So of course I had to go check it out even though I was really tired and would have rather stayed in bed. I had to go and make sure I wasn't crazy.

STRIDER

So? Are you?

AEHLEX

What? Crazy?

(laughs)

Yeah, but that's beside the point.

They both laugh.

AEHLEX

No but seriously, sure enough I'm standing in the

hallway talking to Vinnie the door guy and guess

who shows up alone and exactly at midnight.

STRIDER

That's freaky.

Aehlex begins stretching and yawning. She is also shaking her arms and rolling her neck

AEHLEX

Tell me about it.

STRIDER

Do you think that he knows?

AEHLEX

I don't know. I really don't think so though. Although

we did both seem kinda wierded out.

Aehlex keeps stretching and yawning. Shaking her arms and rolling her neck with a perplexed
look on her face.

STRIDER

Are you alright? What's going on?

AEHLEX

I'm not sure. All of a sudden I feel a little weird.

I'm all tingly. I almost feel like I'm about to start

floating.

Aehlex suddenly begins to channel "aliens". She is also completely conscious of what is going on
and involved in the conversation. When channeling, Aehlex is mainly still with slow reserved
movement. When not channeling she is herself.

CHANNEL

Greetings. We are honored to be here.

AEHLEX

(surprised)

Oh. I guess I'm channeling. This is new.

173

STRIDER

Finally! What took you guys so long?

AEHLEX

They are all in different places yet in the same

room at the same time. It's like a room without

walls. It's hard to describe. I can see their symbol.

It says: (pause) Intergalactic Federation of Light.

STRIDER

Yep. Those are our people.

Aehlex frowns and shakes her head.

STRIDER

What's wrong?

AEHLEX

They are all trying to speak at once.

(to the Intergalactic Federation of Light)

You guys are gonna have to speak one at a time.

(pause) Oh. They are telling me that Eddie is coming.

Suddenly Strider's neighbor Eddie calls his name from inside Josephs bedroom downstairs.

Eddie is Hispanic about 5'7" with dark hair and dark eyes. He is 25.

EDDIE

Strider!

Aehlex and Strider look at each other and smile.

STRIDER

What's up?

Eddie climbs up the stairs to the loft and sticks his head thru the hatch. He sees Aehlex.

EDDIE

(smiles)

Hey Aehlex.

AEHLEX

(smiles)

Hey.

EDDIE

(to Strider)

Can I borrow Seth Speaks and also that Dan

Millman book?

STRIDER

Which one? The life you were born to live.

EDDIE

Yeah. I want to show 'em to someone. I'll bring

'em back tomorrow.

STRIDER

Sure.

Strider grabs the books from a small bookcase within arms reach of where he is sitting.

EDDIE

What are you guys up to?

AEHLEX

(casually)

Oh, not much. I just started channeling for the first

time in my life about two minutes ago. That's all.

Strider laughs.

EDDIE

Are you serious?

AEHLEX

I'm being told that you don't know your father but

that it is better that way.

EDDIE

(surprised)

I've never told you that!

STRIDER

You've never told me that either.

AEHLEX

Your father was not the nicest guy.

EDDIE

Was?

AEHLEX

(pause)

They are not answering. I think that's all you needed

to know.

EDDIE

(a bit shocked)

Ok then. I'll see you two later. Thanx for the books.

Eddie leaves.

                    AEHLEX
              (smiles)

        Think that freaked him out?

                    STRIDER
              (smiles)

        Just a little.

They both laugh.

                    STRIDER
              (to the federation)

        So when are you guys gonna come see us?

                    AEHLEX
              (to the federation)

        Yeah, we know that you're real but being in these 3D

        bodies we need physical proof otherwise our logical

        minds simply won't except this reality. But you already

        know that, don't you?

                    STRIDER

        We'll go out to the desert to meet you.

                    AEHLEX

        No. I'm not going all the way out to any desert for

        some entities that might not show up. Especially,

                                                    178

not when we have the ocean right here.

CHANNEL

Ok, see you soon. One month by the lagoon.

AEHLEX

Very good.

STRIDER

Who is that rhyming?

AEHLEX

I don't know but he's very playful. I think that's it.
(pause) Yep, their gone. Shoot! I totally forgot to
ask them about that whole Perry thing that just
happened. I mean if it was them, why would they
use Perry's voice? Oh well Whatever. Alright, I'm
takin' off. I'm Totally wiped. I'll call you tomorrow.

Aehlex climbs down and disappears from the loft.

FADE...

INTERIOR ~ AIRPLANE ~ LAX ~ DAY

Aehlex is sitting by the window reading an article on Hutchinson's disease..

Trent is sitting next to Aehlex also reading a magazine.

AEHLEX

(sighs)

I'll never understand why we allow heinous murderers

to have the death penalty but we won't allow assisted

suicide for the terminally ill. I'm reading this article

about Hutchinson's disease. It's so terrible. There's no

help for these people. They just slowly deteriorate until

they become trapped within their own painful bodies and

eventually die. It's really sad and incomprehensible.

TRENT

That is sad. Most of the time murderers prefer death

over prison. So were just giving them what they want

anyway.

AEHLEX

Exactly, and we don't really know what happens when

we die. I think that all murderers should have to live

in prison together. You know murderers in one prison.

Rapist in another. Let them kill and rape each other if

that's what they want to do. Then we all get what we want.

TRENT

Yeah. No kidding. Well, it's definitely cheaper to keep

them alive.

AEHLEX

Well, anyway you look at it. Killing for killing is just

plain stupid. I think It sends a really bad message. But

that's just my opinion.

TRENT

I totally agree.

Trent continues to look at his magazine.

Aehlex moves her seat back.

AEHLEX

Madness! It's all madness! I'm going to sleep.

Aehlex closes her eyes.

INTERIOR ~ ALIEN ARCHIVES ~ VENICE, CA ~ DAY

There are shelves upon shelves of hundreds of different UFO videos.

Aehlex surprises strider at work. She is wearing a 70's style polyester shirt and pants

Strider is on the telephone with his back to Aehlex while she is patiently standing in the door way.

STRIDER

I'll find out and call you back. (pause) Bye.

AEHLEX

(sarcastic humor)

There's no such things as aliens!

Strider turns around in surprise.

STRIDER

Your back! How was Holland?

Gets up and hugs Aehlex.

AEHLEX

(annoyed)

Yeah, I'm back.

(happy)

It was awesome! As always. And I met a really hot
guy who actually had a clue.

STRIDER

Someone with a clue. Wow! Sounds like you had fun.
By the way, I've been meaning to ask you if you've
seen your friend Bryan around lately.

AEHLEX

Not lately. He called me a few weeks ago and told
me that he might be going out of town for a while.
Why?

STRIDER

I have something for him.

AEHLEX

Next time I hear from him, I'll let him know. So,
has it been a month yet?

STRIDER

(gruffly)

No. Three weeks.

AEHLEX

I knew you were keeping track you Virgo.

STRIDER

Oh, by the way these are for Jeanette.

Strider hands Aehlex two UFO video's.

AEHLEX

Right on. Thank You

STRIDER

What are you up to?

AEHLEX

I'm on my way to work and just thought I'd stop

by and let you know I'm back. I guess I needed

to pick these up too. Well, get back to work I'm

outta here. Call me Later.

INTERIOR ~ THE MYSTIC EYE BOOKSTORE ~ DAY

Alexis is standing behind the Attic counter speaking with a psychic. She is still wearing the 70's

style polyester shirt and pants as well as a blue apron that says The Mystic Eye, with a large front

pocket.

The psychic is standing on the other side of the counter where purchases are made.

PSYCHIC

When my 3 o'clock appointment

gets here, can you just tell her...

The schizoid approaches the counter, interrupts the psychic & points at Aehlex.

SCHItZOID

(angrily)

Your reign of terror is over!

AEHLEX

(sarcastically)

Really? Wow. I think that may be the best thing anyone

has ever said to me.

The psychic looks at the man strangely and walks away.

Now the schizoid and Aehlex are the only ones in the Attic.

SCHIZOID

I came into this store the other day, you walked by

me wearing that Star of David and my feet swole up.

Aehlex just stares at the man sternly for about ten seconds in silence.

Suddenly the man swiftly walks around the counter.

Aehlex see's him coming for her and tries to make it out the Attic door but is met by the schizoid

before she can get out the door. Now the two of them are face to face and only inches apart.

SCHIZOID

Come here I've got something or you.

The schizoid quickly pulls out a giant torch lighter, points it at Aehlex's stomach and lights it.

At the very same moment Aehlex jumps back and quickly leaps over the counter and runs into the

main section of the bookstore.

AEHLEX

Fuck'n aye dude! That guy in the Attic just tried

to light me on fire.

Jonahs walks over to the Attic. He is also wearing an apron.

AEHLEX

(to herself)

Man I gotta quit this job.

EXTERIOR ~ TOPANGA CYN AND PCH/MALIBU, CA ~ SUNSET ~NIGHT

TITLE ~ Topanga Canyon ~ November 1998

MUSIC: Swan Lee's song 'Social Disease' is playing

Aehlex, Strider, & Charlie are walking up a cement drainage pipe on the side of a hill. Aehlex's two dogs, Honey and Sasha Fu are also with them off leash.

Charlie is leading, she has short blonde hair and green eyes.

Strider is walking behind Charlie, wearing a tan colored poncho.

Aehlex is walking behind both Charlie and Strider.

Honey is walking with Aehlex while Sasha is dragging behind.

AEHLEX

> (turns around)
> Come on Mr. Fu!

They sit on a mountain cliff over looking the ocean high above PCH just past Topanga Canyon.

Aehlex is sitting in the middle looking at the ocean.

Strider is sitting to the left of Aehlex looking at the sky.

Charlie is sitting to the right of Aehlex playing with a stick in the dirt.

Honey is lying next to Aehlex while Mr. Fu is running around the mountain close by.

Strider

(skeptical)

They're not gonna show up.

AEHLEX

Give em a chance. The sun's not even down yet.

CHARLIE

Who's not gonna show up?

Strider and Aehlex just look at each other.

AEHLEX

(Charlie)

Ok , there's something we gotta tell ya.

CHARLIE

What?

AEHLEX

I know you think that you brought us here just to hang

out but strider and I kinda have an appointment tonight.

CHARLIE

What do you mean?

AEHLEX

I should probably start from the beginning. Um. Ok.

Sometime during 1995, I began my UFO education.

CHARLIE

You're not about to tell me that we're here to meet

aliens. Are you?

AEHLEX

Just listen. So anyway, I was taught how to spot them

in the sky. I was shown how to differentiate

between UFO's, stars, satellites, planets and airplanes.

Because UFO's simulate these things.

CHARLIE

Why?

AEHLEX

Because that way it's easier for them to drift thru

our skies unnoticed. At the time I was living alone
& I began to notice that a certain star would appear
and disappear at the same times each night while the
other stars would remain still. This one particular star
also did things that the others never did. It shot out little
orange lights and hovered. It also communicated with
other red lights in the sky. I assume that these were
smaller related vessels. I didn't know much about UFO's
at the time but I did have a firm belief in the probability
of their existence.

CHARLIE

How old were you?

AEHLEX

I was 18 or 19. I remember watching them while
outside on my balcony. One night I asked, "what
do you want from us? Why can't you just leave us
alone?" That's very funny to me now. Anyway I
turned around to go inside after asking the strange
star that question and before I could get both feet
in the door I heard a loud mail voice in my head
say, "it's an integral part of being." I repeated
what I had just heard a couple of times aloud. I
ran to the dictionary to look up the word integral
because I didn't know what it meant.

CHARLIE

(curiously)

What does it mean?

AEHLEX

It means, necessity for completeness. The last thing
I expected to receive was a response. From that point
on I trusted that the strange stars were not stars at all.

Strider laughs.

AEHLEX

A month ago, I channeled for the first time in my life.
And we agreed to meet by the ocean in 30 days. So
earlier when you asked us if we wanted to come here,
we figured that it was to meet them.

CHARLIE

OK.

Aehlex looks over at Strider who is watching the planes go by.

AEHLEX

Why are you so quiet?

STRIDER

I'm just studying the flight paths of these airplanes.

AEHLEX

Good thinkin.

EXTERIOR ~ TOPANGA CYN AND PCH/MALIBU, CA ~ SUNSET ~NIGHT

As soon as the sun goes down Aehlex spots what looks like a star moving in the sky directly over their heads.

AEHLEX

(pointing)

There's one.

The star stops hovering.

Strider proceeds to argue with Aehlex about it.

STRIDER

That's a star.

AEHLEX

No it's not. It was hovering all around before I

pointed to it.

STRIDER

That's a star look I'll measure it's distance from that
planet and then we'll watch it.

Strider puts his right hand up as if to measure it with his thumb and index finger, against the other

stars in the sky. At that very moment all the stars over our their heads fall out of the sky and

disappear.

AEHLEX

Crazy! Except for that one, I thought the rest were
all stars.

Then Aehlex hears a male voice say, "that was the first of 80" telepathically.

AEHLEX

I've just been told that this is the first of eighty.

Many different types of craft appear begin to appear directly in front of them over the ocean,

approximately one half block away.

Aehlex, Strider and Charlie are all looking in different directions while trying to get the others

attention.

CHARLIE

(pointing to the right of the sky)

Oh wow. Look at that one.

STRIDER

(excited and pointing to the left of the sky)

That is so cool! Look at that.

AEHLEX

(looking straight ahead)

Look at that thing. What's that thing?

Aehlex is pointing at one very odd craft. It looks like one of those 4th of July sparklers. It is long and skinny stick like craft which had big bright sparklers at each end. We've all seen a similar effect on airplanes but those sparklers flash, these do not.

AEHLEX

I'm sure glad we watched the flight paths for a
while before the sun went down.

STRIDER

Yeah. Now we know that these craft are not flying

anywhere near the flight paths.

They see what looks like the mother of the stealth bomber. They also see a large craft that looks

exactly like a rocket ship except that it flew side-ways like an airplane. They see one really large

round ship with lights all around it. So many craft. There are also orbs, little robotic spies.

Once the activity in the sky stops, Strider walks away into the darkness.

Aehlex starts looking around as if she is seeing things in her peripheral vision.

AEHLEX

(to Charlie)

I just realized that some of them are down here with us.

I can feel it. Man, It's getting cold out here.

CHARLIE

Let's move around.

Suddenly Aehlex, Charlie and the dogs who are all standing, begin to see outlines of invisible

people zipping around them. All four heads whip around in the same directions as they are all

seeing the same things.

AEHLEX

That's them.

CHARLIE

They look like invisible outlines

of people.

AEHLEX

They're energy vibrates so much higher than ours.

That's why they look like that to us. Normally we

wouldn't see them at all but our own energies are

slightly elevated right now just from having this

experience.

Strider has been gone for several minutes and Aehlex begins to worry about him.

AEHLEX

Where the hell did Strider go?

(yells)

Strider! Strider!

Suddenly Aehlex, Charlie and the dogs hear footsteps.

AEHLEX

Strider, is that you?

No response.

Strider!

Suddenly the girls see a figure coming toward them. The dogs begin to growl because It looks as if the mountain is coming toward them.

CHARLIE

Are you seeing this?

AEHLEX

Yep.

The closer the figure got the clearer it became. Strider who is wearing a tan poncho, looks as if he has camouflaged with the natural surroundings and the mountain.

Strider is smiling deviously.

AEHLEX

(sarcastically)

Dude! Why didn't you answer me? You jerk, you

scared us.

CHARLIE

You totally morphed with the mountain it was crazy

it looked like the mountain was walking toward us.

They begin wandering around the mountain.

While walking around they begin to notice that certain spots are much warmer than others.

Strider is walking ahead of the ladies. He stops. Backs up 2ft and then walks backwards 2ft. He does it twice.

STRIDER

You guys check it out. It's much warmer over here

than over there.

AEHLEX

What?

Charlie and Aehlex walk over to where Strider is standing.

CHARLIE

Oh my God, you're right.

AEHLEX

That's weird!

They all walk in and out of the warm spots a few times. Then stand in it for a few moments.

198

AEHLEX

This is so cool or I should say warm.

(looks up)

Thank you guys.

(to Strider)

I was just complaining about being cold.

CHARLIE

Wait, now it's cold again.

AEHLEX

(looks up)

Very funny.

They all begin walking again and come to another warm spot and stop.

STRIDER

Here's another one.

AEHLEX

Nice.

They stand there for only a few seconds before Aehlex telepathically hears "there is someone waiting to meet you at the top of the hill".

EXT ~ SIDE OF A MOUNTAIN ~ TOPANGA/MALIBU, CA ~PCH ~ NIGHT

                              AEHLEX

        Hmm. You guys come here.

Without explanation Aehlex begins to lead Strider, Charlie and the dogs up a the hill and begin

walking up it. There is no path, bushes, brush and poison Ivy. About a twenty-five feet up,

Aehlex stops and turns around.

                              STRIDER

            Damn it!!!

Aehlex jumps.

                              AEHLEX

        What?

                              STRIDER

        They just told me that it was up to you if we would

        Go and you stopped and turned around.

                              AEHLEX

            (smiles)

        I'm sorry. I'm not in the mood to climb up the side

        of that hill. Besides there's poison ivy in those bushes.

Voice over as they walk back down the hill.

NARRATION: AEHLEX'S VOICE OVER   *"There was poison Ivy in those bushes and I*

really wasn't in the mood but the truth of the matter is that I was more concerned about whether

or not my friends and I could handle any more excitement that evening. I am also a Leo and just

don't think that I should have to climb mountains to meet anyone. What can I say, sometimes I'm

a little bit of a diva."

INTERIOR ~ ALIEN ARCHIVES ~ DAY

TITLE ~ Two days later

Aehlex and Strider walk into Alien Archives and approach Strider's boss' desk.

SFX: The phones are ringing off the hook.

Strider's boss is tall and casual with long crazy curly hair.

STRIDER'S BOSS

I'm so glad you're here. We've been getting a lot of

reports all day from people in the Topanga/ Malibu

area, about strange activity in the sky on Friday night.

AEHLEX

(smiles)

Nice. That rocks!

Aehlex and Strider just look at each other and laugh.

STRIDER'S BOSS

What's so funny?

STRIDER

We know. We were there. I'll tell you all about it

in a sec.

(to Aehlex)

Thanx for the ride.

AEHLEX

Acuna Matada.

Walks away.

INTERIOR ~ THE MYSTIC EYE BOOKSTORE ~ THE ATTIC ~ DAY

MUSIC: The White Stripes song 'In the cold cold night is playing'

TITLE ~ 1 month later

Aehlex is sitting on a stool behind the counter in the Attic.

Strider and his friend Paul walk into the Attic from the Attic's front door to the left of where Aehlex is standing.

AEHLEX

Hey you guys. What's up?

Both Strider and Paul walk behind the counter and stand to the right of Aehlex.

Strider is to Aehlex's right.

Paul is to Strider's right. Paul is always skeptical about Strider and Aehlex's UFO sightings.

Suddenly a very tall aprox. 6'1", thin Caucasian looking woman comes around the corner from the main side of the store. She is bald, wearing sunglasses, a white wife beater, khaki shorts and sandals. She is also holding a stack of flyers.

The bald woman heads straight for Aehlex. As she began to speak to Aehlex she takes off her glasses.

Although the bald woman's eyes are shaped like a human's, they are anything but. As a matter of fact the inside looks like the eyes of a big oval head Grey alien. Where we have pink her eyes were charcoal Grey. There was no white around her eyes either. They were a filmy black color with a slimy looking texture. (The woman actually looks like the android laying on the medical table in the Step Ford Wives trailer)

Strider and Paul are looking at the bald woman in wonder and silence.

Aehlex pretends not to notice.

BALD WOMAN

Can I put a flyer up on your bulletin board?

AEHLEX

(casually responds)

No, I'm sorry that's only for our psychics. People ask all the time.

BALD WOMAN

Thank you.

The bald woman puts on her sunglasses and leaves.

PAUL

I'm hungry.

Aehlex and Joseph say the same exact thing in unison.

STRIDER & AEHLEX

(to Paul)

Woe! Woe! Woe! Back it up!

STRIDER

You can't tell us that you didn't just see that!

PAUL

(uncertain)

Ya, but...

AEHLEX

But what? Dude you never believe anything we tell

you. You finally see it with your own eyes and you

still don't believe it. Whatever! That was definitely

not Hollywood makeup. I grew up around the biggest

special effects guy in Hollywood and that was not his

work.

STRIDER

Where do you think she's from.

AEHLEX

Not here. Although she is definitely half human.

STRIDER

She could be Neflum.

AEHLEX

Did anyone get a look at her flyers?

Paul shakes his head no.

STRIDER

No! Damn it! I was too mesmerized by her eyes.

AEHLEX

I thought it was strange that you guys came back
and stood behind the counter. Now I get it. You
needed to be there to see her eyes.

STRIDER

You're right. I didn't even notice that we did that.

PAUL

I was just following Strider.

EXTERIOR ~ THE MYSTIC EYE BOOKSTORE ~ THE ATTIC DOORWAY ~ LATER SAME DAY

Aehlex is sitting outside taking a break when she spots the bald woman walking with a bald man and a tiny Chihuahua. They are across the street walking down Main Street in Venice toward Rose Ave.

The bald man and woman are both wearing identical outfits and they look like carbon copies of each other. Both the man and woman are the exact same height and build. Both bald. The only difference is that you can tell one is female because she has breasts. They appear to be acting as if they are boyfriend and girlfriend, holding hands.

AEHLEX

(to herself)

They look like identical twins. We don't have male
and female identical twins on this planet.

Aehlex begins speaking to them telepathically.

AEHLEX

(telepathically)

I know that you can hear me. I know that you can
read my thoughts.

At that very moment the bald man and woman both stop, turn toward Aehlex and look at her, in unison.

                              AEHLEX

                         (telepathically)

                  Thank you. Thank you very much.

The bald man and woman walked away.

**INT ~ AEHLEX'S CAR ~ OCEAN WALKWAY & NAVY ST. ~ SANTA MONICA, CA ~
DAY**

TITLE ~ One week later

Aehlex is sitting in her car at lunch with Jeanette

They are eating in silence parked on Navy St. in front of the ocean exactly two blocks away from
the Mystic eye.

Aehlex continuously looks around and in her mirrors. She see's that no one is to be found in any
direction. She looks into her rear view mirror and into the green sedan parked directly behind her.
The moment that her eyes shift away from the rear view mirror a car door slams. Aehlex looks
back up at the rear view mirror.

The tall bald woman is standing near the driver side door of the green sedan.

The tall bald man and the tiny Chihuahua dog are standing on the passenger side of the green
sedan. He slams the door and slowly walks down the sidewalk toward the beach.

The woman casually walks by Aehlex's side of the car in the street and gives her a glance.

                              AEHLEX

                    (perplexed)

              Jeanette, did you hear those car doors open?

                              JEANETTE

              No. I just heard doors slam.

Aehlex watches the bald man and woman.

                              AEHLEX

              Me too. Weird. Do you remember me telling you

              about those people from earlier this week?

                              JEANETTE

                    (eating)

              Yes.

                              AEHLEX

              That's them.

                              JEANETTE

              (looks up)

              Noooo. What do you think they want?

AEHLEX

I don't know. I think they want to talk

to me but either they aren't ready to talk

to me yet or they don't think I'm ready to

talk to them. Either way as long as they

keep walkin we'll be alright.

The bald man and woman and dog turn right around the corner.

FADE OUT...

EXT~ AEHLEX'S BEDROOM WINDOW~ VENICE, CA ~ DAWN

Aehlex is out of her body hovering above her bedroom window. She looks like a ghost. It is very blue outside and the sun is just starting to rise. She sees a young man about five feet away from her window.

INT ~ AEHLEX'S BEDROOM ~ VENICE, CA ~ DAWN

Aehlex is laying in bed asleep. She quickly opens her eye's and sits straight up in her bed. She sees that her animals are calm and sleeping.

AEHLEX

(whispers)

Was I dreaming?

SFX: Suddenly Aehlex hears tapping and scratching at her window as if someone is trying to get in.

Her animals do not react.

AEHLEX

(in her deep morning voice)

You have ten seconds to get the fuck away from my

window!

SFX: Aehlex hears the man scurry through the bushes. She looks out the window and sees the back of the man's head. He is the same man whom Aehlex saw moments before while hovering out of body.

Sasha finally starts to bark.

AEHLEX

Sure, now you bark. I can't believe you guys slept

through that? That was really weird.

EXTERIOR ~ NORTH ON LINCOLN BLVD ~ VENICE, CA ~ DAY

TITLE ~ CHRISTMAS DAY 1998

MUSIC: De La soul's song 'Buddy'.

Aehlex is driving and singing to De La soul's song 'Buddy'. Her cell phone rings. She turns down the music and answers the phone. It's Bryan.

AEHLEX

Shalom. Merry Christmas.

BRYAN

Where you at?

AEHLEX

Is this Bryan?

BRYAN

Yes, it is.

AEHLEX

Where you at? Are you back?

BRYAN

Yep. I have a surprise for you.

AEHLEX

You do. What is it?

BRYAN

Can you meet me on 7th and Flower Right now?

AEHLEX

Sure thing. I'll be there in less than five minutes.

EXTERIOR ~ 7TH & FLOWER VENICE, CA ~ CHRISTMAS DAY ~

MUSIC: De La Soul's 'Buddy' is still playing.

Aehlex pulls into an alley on the north East corner of 7TH & Flower next to a small poor church. She parks and gets out of her car. There is a small white motor home on the church property.

Bryan is sitting in his wheel chair in front of the motor home.

AEHLEX

(excited & pointing at the motor home)

Is this yours?

BRYAN

Yep. A really nice lady just gave it to me.

AEHLEX

No way, dude that's awesome! I'm so happy for you.

What a great surprise!

BRYAN

(smiles)

That's only part of the surprise.

AEHLEX

(curious)

Ok.

Bryan smiles and gets out of his wheelchair.

Aehlex covers her mouth with her hand in shock.

AEHLEX

(happy)

Your walking again! Oh my God! So, that's where

you've been. No wonder you were so secretive about it.

Bryan gives her a hug.

                    BRYAN

Merry Christmas.

                    AEHLEX

        (shaking her head)

I honestly could not have asked for a better Christmas

present. I can't wait to tell everyone.

                    BRYAN

And I know you will.

                    AEHLEX

You got that right.

Aehlex looks directly at the camera and smiles.

FREEZE FRAME   **FADE TO BLACK…..**

Dedication

Mom, Dad, Arnold Schwarzenegger, , Perry Farrell, Marvin Gaye, Jezo, Kat, Grandma, Andy Dick, Jaeneen & Eric, Jason Pauling and family, Aunt Pat & Ryan, Betty Lou Henson, Josh and family, Kev & Megan, Diana, Myra Davis, Rose Maria King, Bob King and Megan King, Frank Lawson, Justin Sandler, Ricky Perrgrino, Gerrardo, Stacie, Mitch, Noni & Paul, Marvin Wadlow, Kevin, Ace, Gardner Cole, Tony, Charlee, Strider, Neal, Paul, Sam, Kim D., Samiah, Sheera & Maggie, Arno, Zorro, Ms. Honey Sunshine, Tracy (Sheba) Collins, Mr. Sasha Fu, Cayce (Kayceo), Mohe, Gigiloo, Lion, King, Evee, The Warlock, Bruce, Robert S. Marta, Mary & The Psychic Eye Bookshop, Jonah, "The Psychic Eye" psychics, Jennifer & Sean, Shane , Adam, Little Steve, Steve Gilmore, Egypt, Faith, Lisa, Jane's Addiction, Smashing Pumpkins, Don Manuel, all of my spirit guides, guardian angels, my parking fairies, The Intergalactic Federation of Light, The family of light, The Pleiadians, Gaea, the Sun, Love, all the good people in the world & The Creator!

R.I.P.-We miss you Betty Lou   ☺

R.I.P. Arno - see you on the otherside

Recommended books

*Seth Speaks ~ The Eternal Validity of the Soul~ Jane Roberts

*The Nature of Personal Reality ~ Jane Roberts

*Bringers of the Dawn ~ Teachings from The Pleiaidians (1992)

~Barbara Marciniak

*Earth ~ Pleiadian keys to the Living Library (1995) ~ Barbara Marciniak

*Family of Light ~Pleiadian tales and lessons in living (1999) ~ Barbara

Marciniak

*The Life you Were Born To live ~ Dan Millman

*The Secret - Rhonda Byrne's discovery of The Secret began with a

glimpse of the truth through a 100 year old book. She went back through

centuries.......

Ink ~ Live Nude Class Drawing~ Paris 96'~ Aehlex

Self Help tips

Its always a great idea to meditate and do yoga but meditation and yoga are not for everybody. A terrific alternative is 20-45 minutes of stretching and slow, deep, breathing every morning &/or night. Keep your thoughts on your breathing and also repeat personal Mantra's ~ (words of encouragement & empowerment) ex: I am smart. I am beautiful. I am powerful. I feel calm. I feel centered. I am conscious and awake. I am successful. I am affluent. Classical music and chanting are also very helpful sounds that will help to clear your mind. You may want to check out "The law of attraction" and "The secret" but be cautious. The law of attraction is real and it works. Once one has mastered the law of attraction, you will see that which you have created emerge more quickly. However, most of us must change our core beliefs and learn to understand and control our thoughts and emotions more before truly being successful conscious creators of our experience and that takes time and patience.

Final Thoughts

Rental history reports

Why do we allow landlords to invade our privacy? Instead of credit
report checks we should have rental history reports. We can pay our rent
on time every month for twenty years and no one would know or care.
Let's say we fall on hard times, get laid off from our job and end up
getting evicted (after 20 years of perfect payment). Now your credit is
hurting and you cannot find a decent place to live because no one
outside of gang ridden neighborhoods will rent to you. It's not fair
and it is an invasion of privacy not to mention the fact that credit
checks while apartment hunting also hurts your credit. Most people miss
payments on their bills so that they can pay the rent and keep a roof
over their heads.. so credit checks really don't give landlords any
information which they need. Evictions can go onto the rental history
reports as well your credit score and any felony convictions.

Mandatory paternity testing

After everything I went thru with my father's estate I found it hard to
believe that a mother is allowed to put any man's name on a birth
certificate without any physical proof. Now that DNA testing is so

readily available, it seems dumb not to make paternity testing mandatory for birth certificates. And now with the Death of Anna Nicole Smith, the perils of not protecting the importance and authenticity of this most important paper of our lives has been brought to our attention in a big way. Hopefully we will make some changes.

Bank Regulation

We the people need to be better protected from banks and corporations. There must be much stricter and much better bank regulation in America!

Homeland

We must open up some of the vast and unused Federal Land for the homeless. Example: Take 20 acres in the California Desert (within an hour of L.A.) Set up hundreds of sturdy, clean and inexpensive geo~ dome homes. Also have a building with a cafeteria, showers, re-hab, mental institution, school, drug counselors and therapists. Build a train from Downtown to 'the Homeland'. Trains run 8x a day (could be solar or natural energy). Establish a homeless curfew where they must be off the streets at night, since it is illegal to sleep on the street. They are free to come and go as they please as long as they return to 'the Homeland' or a shelter at night. If they continue to attempt to sleep on city streets then they will be arrested and taken back to 'the Homeland' where they must stay for 30 days before being allowed to leave again. Have a task force of police specifically for homeless curfew offenders. Give the homeless an address, motivation and incentives to return to the Homeland and help to better their lives. If mentally and emotionally capable most will do better with some stability and assistance.

Incentives and Prison

I also feel that we must take care of our people and not just throw them into prisons or onto death row. I think Incentives would be a good way to get sex offenders and violent criminals to seek help before committing a crime. Make serial sex offenders and violent serial murderers stay in solitary confinement for life. Don't give them the opportunity or satisfaction of hurting anyone else. Make them watch and listen to stuff they don't like in their cells 24/7. Give them self help books and things they would only read out of complete boredom. Not being able to socialize or have contact with other inmates makes it 100 times harder to smuggle drugs into the prisons or run gangs from Death Row. Separate the violent criminals from the non-violent and keep them in entirely different prisons. STOP putting children in adult prisons, period! The punishment must fit the crime and too many good people who have made stupid mistakes end up in our horrible and violent prisons. My idea's for all of these things are much more detailed, well thought and complicated than outlined here. I just want to throw out these general idea's.

Quote

"We should have much more respect for homosexuals. Not only are they too God's creatures, but many gay people help control the population and often care for our orphan children ". Aehlex

www.ingramcontent.com/pod-product-compliance
Lightning Source LLC
Chambersburg PA
CBHW031835090426
42741CB00005B/256